P9-CDE-483

Introducing the Practice of Ministry

Kathleen A. Cahalan

LITURGICAL PRESS
Collegeville, Minnesota

www.litpress.org

Amazon 8/2013

$13.73

Cover design by Ann Blattner. Courtesy of istockphotos.com.

Scripture texts in this work are taken from the *New Revised Standard Version Bible* © 1989, Division of Christian Education of the National Council of the Churches of Christ in the United States of America. Used by permission. All rights reserved.

© 2010 by Order of Saint Benedict, Collegeville, Minnesota. All rights reserved. No part of this book may be reproduced in any form, by print, microfilm, microfiche, mechanical recording, photocopying, translation, or by any other means, known or yet unknown, for any purpose except brief quotations in reviews, without the previous written permission of Liturgical Press, Saint John's Abbey, P.O. Box 7500, Collegeville, Minnesota 56321-7500. Printed in the United States of America.

	2	3	4	5	6	7	8	9

Library of Congress Cataloging-in-Publication Data

Cahalan, Kathleen A.
    Introducing the practice of ministry / Kathleen A. Cahalan.
        p.   cm.
    Includes bibliographical references and index.
    ISBN 978-0-8146-3169-0 — ISBN 978-0-8146-3928-3 (e-book)
    1. Pastoral theology.   2. Church work.   I. Title.
    BV4011.3.C34 2010
    253—dc22
                                                    2010017074

Introducing the Practice of Ministry

Contents

Preface

Introducing the Practice of Ministry is a book intended for people who are discerning a call to ministry in both Catholic and Protestant communities, students who have entered ministry studies at the undergraduate or graduate level, as well as members of parishes and congregations who want to understand the call to ministry and its relationship to Christian discipleship. No single book can say everything about ministry, which is a large and complex topic. It is important at the outset that I clarify what the book attempts to bring to our conversations about ministry.

Over the past ten years I have taught a course titled Introduction to Pastoral Ministry at Saint John's University School of Theology·Seminary, a Catholic and Benedictine school that educates both ordination candidates (priesthood and diaconate) and lay ecclesial ministers. In the course students explore six basic questions about ministry: Who is the minister? What is ministry? Why do we practice ministry? Where and when does ministry take place? How do we practice ministry? Presently, there is no book that introduces students to these six questions in their entirety, and I'm sorry to say this book does not either.

But several questions have become particularly interesting for me, and they serve as the focus of this book. First, what do ministers do that is unique to ministry? In other words, what constitutes the practice of ministry as a vocation and profession in the postmodern world that is continuous with, and rooted in, the long Christian tradition? Second, why is there ministry in the church? What is a rationale for ministry that is both consistent with the Scriptures and tradition and compelling for people today as they explore and take up this vocation? Exploring the "what" and "why" questions led me to ask a more difficult question: is ministry a distinctive vocation and practice that some are called to, or do all Christians participate in the call to ministry, as we commonly hear today in many churches? In other words, who is the minister in the Christian community and how is that vocation identified, recognized, and formed in practice? Oftentimes answers to this question turn immediately to roles or offices such as bishop, pastor, priest, or deacon with the accompanying discussion of the meaning of ordination and who can be ordained. I have put this question aside here, not because it is unimportant, but because I wanted to answer the question "who is the minister" through another route—that of charism and practice. If ministry is a particular vocation, what charisms or gifts from God's Spirit form the theological basis of a distinctive set of practices? How can we understand practice as a way of connecting the "who" and "what" and "why" questions about ministry together? The answers to these three questions, as presented in this book, are closely connected—once I attempted to answer one question I was pushed into considering the next.

The first question—what constitutes the practice of ministry—is important to me because it is a question that we can take for granted or often ignore. I began exploring this question because I felt that ministry is a distinctive vocation with distinctive practices, but the traditional way of thinking about ministry, at least in the Catholic context, has not highlighted practice, but rather identity. It is not uncommon, among Catholics, in discerning a call to ministry to first discern a call to religious life or the priesthood: am I called to be a sister? a brother or monk or priest? The prevailing question has been one of identity that is tied to a celibate way of life. Many people who receive a call to ministry have to first discern their identity in relationship to one of these paths. If I know who I am and what my office, role, or status is in the community, then what I do will follow from that position. Identity nearly always precedes and often trumps practice. You can hear this echoed today in the idea that what is essential about Catholic priesthood is *who* the priest is, not *what* he does. In this book, I want to find a way to overcome this long-standing divide between the person and identity of the minister and practice, what the minister does. I think they are deeply connected, and I believe that discerning a vocation to ministry begins with discerning whether a person has the gifts for the practice as much as it does discerning one's state of life. Identity and practice are inextricably intertwined, but how can we explain this theologically?

Today, the discernment about a call to ministry, and the formation of the identity of a minister, arises primarily through engaging in the practice of ministry over time, and not prior to it. Even in the case of ordination candidates (Protestant or Catholic), it seems woefully inadequate to educate and form a person in the identity of pastor or priest and then expect them to lead a community in full-time parish ministry if we have not given them sufficient training in the practices of ministry. Ministers learn ministry over time, from observing ministers in their childhood and youth, trying on different ministerial roles as youth and young adults, attending seminary and learning some basic knowledge, but also when they step out of formal training and ordination to "practice" ministry each and every day. For many ministers today, ordained and lay, the issues of identity and practice are deeply entwined over a lifetime and the discernment about who I am as a minister and what the call means in my life unfolds over the course of engaged practice in multiple contexts of learning and service. The questions about what constitute the central and enduring practices of ministry and how we understand what "practice" means in relationship to ministry are primarily addressed in chapters 3 and 4.

I begin the discussion of ministry with a lengthy analysis of Christian discipleship in chapter 1 and vocation in the Christian life in chapter 2. Ecclesiologists point out that ministry is rooted in baptism and that we need to understand ordination as well as forms of diaconal and lay ministry in relationship to baptismal call and identity. I agree, but I also have come to understand that baptism does not make us all ministers; in other words, baptism is the ground of ministry but not all the baptized are ministers. I began to see that the practices of ministry arise from, directly relate to, and seek to serve the baptismal reality the New Testament calls "discipleship." In other words, baptism initiates us into the life of discipleship. In chapter 1 I explore seven features of discipleship (follower, worshiper, witness, neighbor, forgiver, prophet, and steward), looking closely at the Hebrew Bible and Jesus' teachings. I argue that discipleship forms the core identity and life of the baptized Christian.

But how does this relate to ministry? Chapter 2 explores Paul's theology of charism, the particular gifts of the Holy Spirit that allow us to be graced with a capacity or competence to serve the common good of the community. I link charism to vocation, the call in adulthood to live our whole life (who I am, what I do, and how I live) in relationship to the gift of discipleship and of charisms, the unique gifts each person receives from the Spirit. In chapter 3, I define ministry as the leadership of the Christian community through six practices of ministry (teaching, preaching, leading worship and prayer, pastoral care, social ministry, and administration). Here I argue that ministry is a unique and particular vocation for which some Christians receive charisms related to these six practices. This means that while members of the Body of Christ share a common calling to discipleship, they do not all have a vocation to ministry. All Christians do, however, have vocations to serve the common good, but the charisms they receive for such service are distinctive and unique. Chapter 4 explores the theological grounds for each of the six practices: how Jesus' life and ministry and the Spirit's charisms form the vocational and ecclesial foundation for each practice of ministry. In chapter 5, I link this understanding of vocation and charism to recent theories of practice and explore a theological way of understanding practice as far more than "doing something." Chapter 6 explores how the life of practice within the profession of ministry, over time, shapes and forms a person toward prudence, the goal of wise practice. In chapter 7 I conclude the book with a reflection on Trinitarian practice, the idea that God is constituted by relationship and practices that draw us into communion. I draw on the biblical wisdom tradition and its influence on early Christology and pneumatology to demonstrate one way in which we can understand the life of practice in relationship to the way of wisdom, the way God practices Trinitarian life and community.

The following outlines the major claims of the book:

1. We experience God reaching out to us in relationship through God's "two hands": the power of the Spirit in creation; vivifying, healing, and renewing life by drawing all things into divine communion; and through the incarnation, life and ministry, and death and resurrection of Jesus, the indwelling of the Spirit in our history.

2. Jesus initiates a group of followers to live in a particular way to seek communion with God and neighbor. Discipleship constitutes the fundamental identity, call, and practice of the baptized Christian.

3. All disciples receive charisms that are unique gifts granted by the Spirit. Charisms are the pneumatological foundation of vocation, which includes how I live my life, what service I offer in community, and who I am. They account for the diversity of vocations in the community, all empowered by the Spirit to serve God's mission in the world.

4. Ministry is one vocation among many vocations in the Christian community and is best identified through the charisms for six practices of ministry. These practices are grounded in both the ministry of Jesus as well as the Spirit's ongoing charismatic expression in

human persons throughout ecclesial history. Ministry exists in the church to serve the life of discipleship for the sake of its mission.

5. Ministry is a verb: it is something people do. We can understand ministry as a practice that is social and communal, expressed within a historical tradition, embodied, relational, spiritual, and professional.

6. Ministry is learned over time in and through practice. The professional practice of ministry constitutes the dynamic interaction of what we know, competence in the skill to act, and the moral virtues of the person we are and are becoming. Practice is the integration of doing, knowing, and being.

7. God practices divine communion as three persons in relationship. This divine communion is practiced with all creation. As "Trinity" God is a communion of divine relationality who made us for relationship and communion. The "practices" of God are meant to draw us into deeper communion with one another and the three divine persons.

Each of these claims could constitute a book on their own, but because this is an introductory book for students and church members, I have kept footnotes to a minimum and included a bibliography at the end of each chapter to point out excellent authors and books. The lists will show my theological sources and conversation partners over the past ten years, those who have helped me think through these questions and claims. I am not, however, directly in dialogue or debate with scholars of ministry, Trinitarian thought, or ecclesiology—the scholarly conversation that informs this book is in the background. Rather, the foreground, I hope, is the introduction to a basic way of thinking about discipleship and ministry that can help students discern if they have gifts for ministry and a call to this vocation, as well as to help those who are responsible for calling forth and educating ministers for their practice.

I dedicate this book to the students of Saint John's University School of Theology·Seminary. In our discussions together, each semester over the past ten years, I was pushed to clarify my thinking about the vocation and practice of ministry. I've taught ministry in perhaps one of the most difficult periods in the Catholic community, certainly in modern times. These issues, then, arise from a particular Catholic context, and I rely largely on Catholic sources, but I intend this discussion of ministry to be "catholic" in the best sense of the term, by inviting Protestant and Orthodox Christians to consider these issues for their communities. I am not addressing the identity and vocation of the ordained or lay ecclesial minister, but I hope it will not be difficult to connect the theology of vocation and practice here with those discussions. I believe that sorting out the questions addressed in this book can go a long way to helping discussions about ordination in all Christian churches. I recognize, as well, that various communities use different terms to describe their ministers, such as pastor, priest, deacon, rector, bishop, and lay minister. I am using the category "minister" in the broad sense, as an umbrella term, that hopefully can capture much of the particularity in each tradition's way of naming and identifying various ministers and ministries.

There are many friends and colleagues I wish to acknowledge and thank for accompanying me during the research and writing of *Introducing the Practice of Ministry*: Carol Lytch and Melissa Wiginton, who first heard the sketch of this book many years ago; Dorothy Bass, Jim Nieman, Bonnie Miller-McLemore, Craig Dykstra, Chris Scharen, and Ted Smith, the "Collegeville group," who meet annually to discuss practice, phronesis, and wisdom in theological education; the women of Spirit Search who have accompanied me in the quest for discerning the Spirit's call; Peggy Thompson and Judith Main, two artists who have taught me that book writing can be as beautiful as book making; the staff of Liturgical Press for their expert practice in book editing and production; Bill Cahoy, dean of the School of Theology, as well as colleagues Jeff Kaster, Vic Klimoski, and Barbara Sutton, who have offered continual support and friendship; the support of Lilly Endowment Inc., especially Craig Dykstra, who is unwavering in his commitment to strengthening the church's ministry and theological education; and, finally, my family, for their love and support, especially my husband Donald B. Ottenhoff, who has accompanied me in the writing of this book as a true companion and friend.

Chapter 1

The Call and Practice of
Christian Discipleship

Jesus is clearly a man with a mission. In the opening of Mark's gospel, the first words he speaks are the proclamation: "The time is fulfilled, and the kingdom of God has come near; repent, and believe in the good news" (1:15). The mission that Jesus proclaims is God's mission to all humanity: to know and love God in the here and now, to leave aside sinful ways that keep us from knowing and loving our neighbor and God, to give our life to this good news until God's promises are complete and fulfilled in the end times. Jesus takes up God's mission with his whole life as well as his death and resurrection: he becomes the witness, the sign and the sacrament, of what God is doing in the world. He gives his life to be God's mission and those who heed his call to "follow me" will be asked to give their life to this same *missio Dei*.

Christians believe that God's mission in creation, history, and the future eschaton is made known through the life and story of Jesus of Nazareth and the movements of the Spirit throughout history. The patristic theologian Irenaeus (d. 202 CE) described God's mission as being carried out through God's two hands, one hand the incarnate Jesus Christ and the other hand the Spirit. The image powerfully captures God's active presence in the world: God's mission is divine redemptive love that is actively at work in molding, shaping, and engaging the creation toward the fullness of life, the transformation of all that is into full relationship with God. The Spirit that breathes life into creation is the source of the incarnate Jesus, calls and empowers his life and witness, raises

1

him from the dead, and births the church of his followers into being. Through "the two hands," we can say that God is drawing near and reaching out in multiple ways to embrace all of creation and humanity. Who God is as "trinity" and what God does through the divine "two hands" are one and the same thing: divine love in relationship, communion, and mission.

The Christian claim that God is Trinity, three-persons-in-one, is claiming two fundamental things about who God is. First, it points to the fact that the divine reality is fundamentally relational, that the essence of divine life is a relationship. The second claim is that the Creator, Son, and Spirit share in a perfect communion of relational love, "a perfect communion of gift and reception, identity and openness to the other, communion in relationship and communion in mission," as Stephen Bevans writes.[1] God's very self, if we can use these terms in an analogous way, is relationship and communion. To inquire into God's mission we can say that who God is is what God does. In other words, God's mission is to bring all creation into loving communion and relationship with the divine mystery, its origin, and God's Trinitarian life points to mutual persons in relationship and community, reaching out to draw all creation into this life of divine communion.

Despite humanity's rejection of God's offer for loving communion, the particular history of the Israelites in the Hebrew Bible and the followers of Jesus in the New Testament tell of God's unrelenting love, compassion for the sinner and outcast, healing mercy for the sick and weak, prophetic demand for mercy and justice, and promise of faithfulness until divine reign is final and complete. We can see in Jesus' ministry a persistent dialogue with people to invite them into this loving relationship with God. Jesus' invitation is to become a disciple and to live the life of discipleship. In and through this radically new identity and practice, God's mission becomes embodied in a community that seeks to live in dialogue and response to the call of reconciliation and justice, mercy and love—all the elements essential for mutual relationship that leads ultimately to loving communion. In this chapter, we look at Jesus' call to invite his followers to live in a particular way and practice a particular way of life. In the next chapter, we turn to the Spirit's active presence in the life of these followers.

---

[1] Stephen B. Bevans and Roger P. Schroeder, *Constants in Context: A Theology of Mission for Today* (Maryknoll, NY: Orbis Books, 2004), 348.

Disciples for Mission

"Disciple" is clearly the most prevalent term to identify followers of Jesus in the New Testament. It is mentioned about 260 times in the gospels and Acts of the Apostles. "Disciple" literally means a "pupil" or "learner" (*mathētēs*, from the verb *manthanein*, "to learn") and was used in ancient times to designate a "follower of a great leader," "one who follows after," and "one who learns."[2]

In antiquity the term "disciple" was used in common discourse and was not necessarily a term applied to religious teachers and pupils. In Greek philosophical schools, for example, many teachers had "disciples," though Socrates, Plato, and Aristotle all seem to have refused such titles for themselves and their pupils. The term "disciple" is found only once in the Old Testament, not at all in the Dead Sea Scrolls, and only later finds its way into the Talmud, where it refers to disciples of particular rabbis. The most prominent and common usage in late antiquity of the term "disciple" is found in the canonical accounts of Jesus of Nazareth. Here it refers to people who physically followed Jesus as well as those who take up a way of life that he embodies and teaches. The term "disciple" also refers to followers of other religious leaders such as John the Baptist, the Pharisees, and Moses, all of whom have "disciples" who follow their teachings. It is difficult to know when "disciple" was introduced into Christian vocabulary, but by the time of the writing of the gospels it is clearly the most common way of designating Jesus' followers.

The first name for Christians seems to be one used by Luke in the book of Acts, "those of the Way," which refers to people, primarily Jews, who accepted salvation through Jesus Christ (Acts 9:2; 19:9, 23; 22:4; 24:14, 22). The term "Christian" was then used, probably first in Antioch, to refer to "those of the household of Christ" or "Christ-followers" (Acts 11:26). It was used to distinguish those who followed Jesus, Jew or Gentile, from Jews who did not follow Jesus. Eventually it was adopted by Jesus' followers to refer to themselves (Acts 26:28; 1 Pet 4:16). These three early terms—followers of the Way, Christian, and disciple—accomplished a similar purpose. They identified a person as a member of a group by who they claim as their teacher and the way of life they have taken up in accepting that person's teaching. This amazing teacher was proclaimed

---

[2] John F. O'Grady, *Disciples and Leaders: The Origins of Christian Ministry in the New Testament* (New York: Paulist Press, 1991), 23.

to be Lord and Messiah by followers of "the Way." Christian identity, from the start, was forged in and through relationship and practice.

As much as the gospels are an account of the story of Jesus, accompanied by theological interpretations of the meaning of his life, death, and resurrection, they are also an account of the disciples and a theological interpretation of discipleship. Each author, in a unique way, creates a portrait of the disciples and the meaning of discipleship that is intended to inform readers about who we are to become and what we are to do as disciples. The Christian tradition is born out of the first followers who pass on what they learn from Jesus about discipleship.

Though each of the four gospels has a distinctive way of portraying the disciples, we can discern a common call pattern. When compared to other teachers of his time, Jesus is unique in that he chooses his first group of disciples, rather than the more common practice in which disciples chose their teacher. At the outset of each story, Jesus calls by name a group to follow him. (Oftentimes the Twelve are equated with the disciples, though for each author there are many more disciples than the initial group called the "Twelve.") Perhaps to emphasize the radical change demanded of this call, Mark tells us that this initial group "immediately" left everything and followed (1:17-18). The gospel writers tell us nothing of the agony or difficulty in leaving behind families, jobs, and homes to follow this itinerant preacher, perhaps because Jesus will later emphasize that nothing can stand in the way of following him. In addition to leaving everything behind, discipleship entails a radical conversion.

Clearly the first step of discipleship is responding to the call to follow Jesus. A disciple is a follower first and foremost. But what does following mean? What must a follower learn along the way? Who do we become when we follow Jesus? To be a disciple means learning a way of life that embodies particular dispositions, attitudes, and practices that place the disciple in relationship to, and as a participant in, God's mission to serve and transform the world. In addition, then, to become a follower, disciples are called to be worshipers, to learn what it means to pray and to worship in "Spirit and truth" (John 4:23). To be a disciple means to become a witness to the risen Christ, to tell others the story of what God has done. To be a worshiper and witness means to learn to be a neighbor, not just to kin and friends, but also to the stranger and the enemy. To follow the way of Christ a disciple must become a forgiver, to learn the practice of seeking forgiveness when they do wrong and offering reconciliation when they themselves are wronged. And becoming a neighbor means becoming a prophet, concerned for all the harm and violence that befalls neighbors. And, finally, to be follower is never a solitary or single endeavor. It means being a member of the community of disciples. To nurture and sustain the Body of Christ and all facets of discipleship, disciples are to be stewards of the gifts of creation and "of God's mysteries" (1 Cor 4:1). These seven features—follower, worshiper, witness, forgiver, neighbor, prophet, and steward—are the central aspects of the life of the disciple that I will elaborate here.

Follower

To be a follower means that a person enters into a lifelong process of learning from Jesus, to come to know who and what Jesus is and what Jesus is claiming about God's call to relationship, communion, and mission. As the theology of the adult catechumenate emphasizes, initiation into the Christian community means living in a state of permanent mystery, a lifelong immersion into mystagogy. To be Christ's follower is to embrace Christ as teacher, to seek wisdom and understanding for what the path and cost of discipleship entails, and to be schooled in the paschal mystery of death and new life.

The beginning of discipleship is Jesus' summons, "Follow me" (Matt 4:19). In the call narratives, several important elements can be noted. First, Jesus calls disciples by name, thus establishing a personal relationship with each disciple. And yet disciples are called into a community that accompanies Jesus, and they are most often referred to in the plural, as disciples. In Matthew's gospel, for instance, the names of disciples are not included in stories until chapter 14. It is the case that we do not know a great deal about the twelve disciples or other disciples that join the journey. Disciples, then, have a personal and a communal relationship to Jesus and to each other.

The story of Jesus and the disciples entails roughly two parts. The first part of each gospel tells the story of the disciples schooling in the way of Jesus. They are taught by him through parables and discourses, and they witness a large number of healings and exorcisms. They are eyewitnesses to the full reality of who and what Jesus is: the proclamation of the presence and future coming of God's reign. And during the course of the early part of Jesus' ministry the disciples grow in understanding and faithfulness, with some being called to take up Jesus' ministry of healing, preaching, and teaching.

The second part of the gospel story entails the journey toward Jerusalem and the dynamics at play when Jesus' death and resurrection become the focus of his life and teachings. A drama unfolds in which an increasing number of disciples, along with the crowd, grow weary and leave, and some continue to follow Jesus. An important element in the story is the growing opposition to Jesus from Jewish religious authorities, Roman officials, and his own followers. As the conflicts heighten, the disciples do not always understand Jesus' teaching, they see but do not believe in God's mission proclaimed by him, and they are increasingly weak, ignorant, and hard of heart (Mark 8:14-21). One denies, another betrays, many flee. Following becomes more complex as the path to suffering and death becomes the route, with some disciples who continue to follow, including a few who stand at the foot of the cross, anoint, and bury him.

The gospel writers do not spare the disciples: they paint a realistic picture, not in order to cast blame or put the disciples down, but because they know themselves that discipleship is a difficult path to follow, one that their own communities struggle to embrace and endure. The first followers stand as powerful witnesses in both their faith and their failures. The tensions in discipleship are real: it entails learning, growing, changing, and converting, as well as turning away, failing, doubting, and at times rejecting the summons. It means taking up with a community of friends, brothers and sisters, a new family and household that includes the unclean and sinners. It also means competition, grabbing for power, and attempts at being first. It can mean a growing distinction and conflict from those who do not believe and follow, and yet it entails a call to "make disciples of all nations" (Matt 28:19) and to embrace the whole world as a place for service and mission. The "way" is one of ambiguity, dichotomy, and tensions that are never neatly resolved but that push disciples into an ever deeper and more difficult discernment of what following really means. Jesus teaches disciples what it means to be a perfect "follower" of God's mission and way when he embraces his death and places his trust completely in God.

Worshiper

In the Gospel of Luke, Jesus is portrayed as a man of prayer. In each significant moment of his life—entering his ministry, during ministry, setting out for Jerusalem, facing his death, and hanging on the cross—

Luke portrays Jesus engaged in the act of praying. Jesus becomes the perfect worshiper, a model for how his disciples are to pray and worship. He also teaches his disciples how to pray (Luke 11:2-4; 18:1), teaches them about prayer (Luke 11:5-8, 9-13), and how to become "true worshipers" in "spirit and truth" (John 4:23).

Prayer, for Jesus, is an ongoing dialogue and source of communion with God. Jesus recognizes God as the source of all that is in creation, the source of healing power and authority in his teaching, preaching, and healing ministries. Prayer is an opening of his heart, mind, and soul to this source of divine love and mercy and a willingness to be transformed into the servant that God is calling him to be. In prayer Jesus offers praise and thanksgiving, asks for forgiveness for those who would harm him, and seeks guidance, direction, and support.

Luke portrays Jesus at prayer during his baptism. He receives the empowering gift of the Spirit and hears God's announcement that he is the Beloved One, the one called to carry forth the mission. In the early phase of his ministry, Jesus seeks solitude to pray. We do not know the words he speaks to God, but it is not hard to imagine that Jesus seeks guidance, direction, and rest. He is overwhelmed by the enthusiastic response to his initial teachings (Luke 4:16-30, 43-44) and the healing of unclean spirits and the sick (Luke 4:33-37, 38-39; 5:12-14). In a fairly brief amount of time "a report about him began to reach every place in the region" (Luke 4:37), and Jesus was attracting large crowds (Luke 4:42; 5:15) as well as initial opposition (Luke 4:29). What could all this mean? What was he to do? At several important points along the journey, Jesus turns to prayer as the source of his ministry and life: prior to his calling the Twelve and teaching the Sermon on the Plain (Luke 6:12); when he asks the disciples "who do you say that I am?" and reveals the first passion prediction and its link to discipleship (Luke 9:18-27); at the transfiguration (Luke 9:28); in the garden at Gethsemane (Luke 22:39-46); and on the cross (Luke 23:46). Jesus both prays for his disciples (Luke 22:32) and asks them for their prayers (Luke 22:40). Through prayer, and by the power of the Spirit, Jesus is able to continue the journey from his ministry to Jerusalem and his death.

Jesus fully embodies what it means to be worshiper, offering his disciples a model to follow and imitate. What disciples learn is that prayer is a dialogue that demands total trust and dependence on God, even in the darkest hour when only lament rises to our lips (Mark 15:34). In following Jesus, disciples learn to join him in worshiping God as creator and redeemer, calling upon God as "Abba" (Matt 6:7-15; Luke 11:1-13).

Prayer and worship become immersions into the divine life and mission.

What does it mean to be a worshiper as Christ is a worshiper? The author of the Letter to the Hebrews explains that Christians have to come to a new understanding of what is distinctive about worship now that they stand in relationship to Christ, the High Priest. Christ, who is the Anointed One in his incarnation, takes on all of what it means to be human and becomes, through his death, the High Priest, the "only" priest necessary for Christians as they stand in relationship to God. Christ changes the divine-human relationship by embracing humanity and by transforming humanity's relationship to God, for all now stand *in Christ* in relationship to God. Jesus, we might say, is the "perfect" disciple insofar as he embodies the servant who through obedient love follows the path and drinks of the cup that he must drink. He is a perfect worshiper insofar as he offers his whole self to God in trust and hope, abandoning everything in his life, including his family, friends, and ministry to take up the cross. Christ, as the one true mediator, stands as the door, the gate, and the opening into God, drawing disciples on a path into that same relationship.

Since early times, Christians pray "through Christ our Lord," a phrase that captures the belief that all Christian prayer is prayer in and through Christ to God. This, of course, is what it means to be the Body of Christ, the community joined in Christ's prayer. Disciples are true worshipers when prayer becomes one with Christ's prayer, a prayer of obedient love, a prayer of a servant, of one who will follow, taking up the cup and following the way of the cross. Even when prayer evades our hearts and lips, the Spirit prays in and for the community of disciples united as Christ's body (Rom 8:26-27).

To be a worshiper is to understand human persons as created for worship. As Jesus is the embodiment of worship, disciples are to become worshipers. Disciples are to take up "doxology as a way of life," according to Catherine Mowry LaCugna. Christians are "most fully human when we praise God" and giving glory to God is not only in prayer and liturgy but also with our whole lives. Living in doxology transforms us to live in "right relationship" so that "once we fathom that *everything* is created for the glory of God and not necessarily for our own consumption, this changes how we relate to the totality of the universe."[3]

---

[3] Catherine Mowry LaCugna, *God for Us: The Trinity and Christian Life* (San Francisco, CA: Harper & Row, 1991), 342ff.

Witness

To be a follower and worshiper, a disciple must also become a witness, one who gives voice to the claim that Christ has made on their life. As Jesus is the Word made Flesh, the Word who gives witness to God's mission, each disciple is created in the image of the Word and becomes, in and through the Spirit, a witness to the risen Christ.

To be a witness means to offer a testimony, to proclaim and announce a message. In both the Hebrew Bible and New Testament, to give a witness is related to speaking the truth about what one has seen and what one knows. In the Pentateuch two basic understandings of witness are recorded: injunctions that require two witnesses to give testimony, the firsthand knowledge of a fact or event, in a court of law to ensure justice and fairness (Exod 23:2; Num 5:13; 35:30; Deut 19:15-16), and injunctions against bearing false witness, speaking untruths against a neighbor (Exod 20:16; 23:1; Deut 5:20; 17:6-7; 9:18-19; Job 10:17).

Both the legal and moral traditions point to the essential claim on the witness: to give testimony to the truth about what they know. "Let them bring their witnesses to justify them, and let them hear and say, 'It is true'" (Isa 43:9). The ultimate witness in the Hebrew Bible, of course, is Yahweh, who knows the truth regarding the people's promise to keep the covenant and their words and deeds that repeatedly break the promise (Jer 42:5). In fact, God is often a witness against the people and a witness of the promises people make to each other (Gen 31:50; 1 Sam 12:5-6; 20:23; Mic 1:2; Zeph 3:8; Wis 1:6; Job 16:19). At the climax of his preaching Moses often calls out for heaven and earth to be a witness against the people (Deut 4:20; 30:19), and he even gives them a song as they are about to enter the Promised Land that "will confront them as a witness." He is of course concerned they will forget and turn away from the covenant (Deut 31:19-21). Moses also claims the book as a witness (Deut 31:24-29; Isa 30:8), and Joshua claims the altar as a witness to the covenant (Josh 22:26-28, 34; Isa 19:20). Later in the prophetic tradition, God calls on the prophets and the people to be witnesses of the Lord (Isa 43:9-12; 44:8; 55:4-5; Zeph 3:9).

The legal and moral meanings of bearing witness can be found throughout the New Testament as well.[4] The New Testament writers

---

[4] Two witnesses in a court of law: Matt 18:15-16; 1 Tim 5:19; John 8:17; 2 Cor 13:1; 1 Tim 5:9; Heb 10:28; Rev 11:3. Bearing false witness in a court: Matt 26:60-65; Mark 14:63; Luke 18:20; Acts 6:13. Injunctions against bearing false witness: Mark 10:19; Matt 15:19; 19:18; Luke 18:20.

place emphasis on Jesus as a witness, a witness to the truth at his own trial (Matt 26:60-65), the one who came to give witness to the light (John 1:7), and the one who is a faithful witness (Rev 1:5). Jesus called upon his disciples to follow him as witnesses, just as he bore witness to the Father, so they are called to be a witness to all that God has done through him. Luke begins and ends his gospel with a focus on witness. Luke claims at the outset that the sources of his proclamation are eyewitnesses of the life, death, and resurrection of Jesus (Luke 1:2; 24:48; Acts 1:8), and in the concluding scene, Jesus tells the disciples, "You are witnesses of these things" (Luke 24:48). In the Acts of the Apostles, Luke is concerned to show that the apostles are witnesses to Jesus, living eyewitnesses who can give an account of his death and resurrection (Acts 1:22; 2:32; 3:15; 5:32; 10:39, 41; 13:31). Of course, Paul, who is not an eyewitness, becomes a witness through his direct encounter and conversion, and his own ministry is based on this witness (Acts 23:11; Rom 1:9; 8:16; 2 Cor 1:23; Phil 1:8). Furthermore, for Paul, through baptism into Christ, the Holy Spirit is "bearing witness" through each disciple that they are "children of God" and "heirs in Christ" who will share in his suffering and glory. Together with other disciples, the church becomes a "cloud of witnesses" on which later generations can depend (Heb 12:1).

As the early Christians learned, giving a witness has consequences. Claiming to be a follower of Jesus in public can mean opposition, hardship, imprisonment, and for some, death. The word "martyr" comes from the same Greek root for "witness" and is claimed for those who meet a violent end because of their testimony but are prepared to suffer gladly "for the name." A witness bears by testimony and a martyr by death.

Testimony is also a liturgical act and when disciples worship, they give witness to the truth of God's mission in their lives. Many churches invite people to give testimony in Sunday morning worship or weeknight prayer services. In the free church tradition, for example, a believer describes what God has done in his or her life and is affirmed by the community's response, "Amen!" A believer's story is witnessed through the biblical story. The personal testimony points to the truth of God in human frailty as well as strength in order that each individual life becomes bound to a common story.

Testimony extends outside liturgy as well. It is a form of evangelization that calls disciples to tell the truth to those who may not know or have experienced it. Thomas Long points out that talking about faith is more than expressing what we believe; we talk about faith because "we are always talking ourselves into being Christian." Likewise, the truth

Christians encounter in the gospel compels them to witness to others not just about themselves, but about God. Long states, "To speak about God is to be in relationship to God, which means that speaking about God is more than speaking *about* God; it is also speaking for, in, with, and to God. Authentic speech about God, therefore, can be said to be a form of prayer."[5] And, in that sense, to be a witness is clearly an aspect of being a worshiper.

Neighbor

The love command that guides disciples is stated clearly in the Hebrew Bible and New Testament. When he is asked by the rich young man what is the greatest of all the commandments, Jesus does not hesitate: "The first is, 'Hear, O Israel: the Lord our God, the Lord is one; you shall love the Lord your God with all your heart, and with all your soul, and with all your mind, and with all your strength.' The second is this, 'You shall love your neighbor as yourself.' There is no other commandment greater than these" (Mark 12:29-31; also Matt 22:34-40; Luke 10:25-28; Deut 6:4). On this great law all other commandments, rules, laws, and principles must find their bearing and measure.

In the Old Testament a neighbor was understood to be a person who was a fellow member of the covenant community, similar to a brother or kinsman. "Neighbor" quite literally refers to those who dwell next to or nearby, people who share land, resources, and traditions. Because of this close proximity and the problems and tensions that arise from dwelling closely together, the Israelites had to work out codes of conduct to guide friendly and peaceable neighbor relations. What precisely did living in covenant mean between neighbors? Neighbors were instructed to be honest and fair in financial dealings with each other, not to covet or steal what a neighbor possesses, not to judge a neighbor's actions harshly, and to help a neighbor in need. Conflict between neighbors brought about serious consequences for the whole community, sometimes ending in national catastrophes. Yahweh was believed to be a harsh judge of those who treated their neighbor badly. Prophets' visions of a new age included images of peace between neighbors, an end to war and bloodshed, with joyous feasts where all neighbors would eat together (Isa 11).

[5] Thomas G. Long, *Testimony: Talking Ourselves into Being Christian* (San Francisco, CA: Jossey-Bass, 2004), 7, 11.

Jesus builds his neighbor ethic on the Great Commandment that links love of God and love of neighbor, even going so far as to place this above all forms of temple sacrifice and worship (Mark 12:31-33). Jesus also teaches honesty between neighbors and warns against the hypocrisy of judging neighbors harshly, since a person's sinfulness is as great if not greater than a neighbors, a point Jesus brings home with the humorous image of the speck in the neighbor's eye and the log in the judge's eye (Matt 7:3). But Jesus continually expands and challenges the teaching on neighbor love to the point of emphasizing love of enemies (Matt 5:43-48). In Jesus' community this often meant neighbors who had come to be hated, rejected, and defiled as unclean and unworthy, such as Samaritans, lepers, tax collectors, and prostitutes. In fact, this is a group of neighbors with whom Jesus often shares food and subsequently breaks laws of ritual cleanliness. Through table fellowship with outcasts, Jesus is a witness to "who is my neighbor," a radical display of who God considers to be neighbor.

The type of community that Jesus envisions is one that welcomes all, not discriminating people or groups based on social categories. He envisions a "neighborhood" where people share food and rejoice together in what is lost and found (Matt 18:12-14; Luke 15:3-10). In John's gospel he places the love commandment in the context of the new community that Jesus has formed. Here Jesus calls the disciples "friends," bound to him not as servants or by family ties, but because he has chosen them to follow him together (John 15:12-17). And for Paul it is the bond in and through Christ that makes neighbors into the Body of Christ (1 Cor 12:12-31). Jesus tells his disciples to preach the gospel to the ends of the earth, and early disciples realize that they must take the gospel into neighborhoods beyond Israel where Gentiles abide. In fact the early "disciples really do not fully *recognize* themselves as church—a separate reality from Judaism—until they recognize that they are called to a mission that has as its scope 'the ends of the earth' (Acts 1:8)."[6]

Forgiver

If upholding the great commandment of neighbor love is difficult, certainly one of the most complicated aspects of discipleship is to learn how to become a forgiver. Practicing forgiveness and reconciliation bring a disciple face-to-face with their wrongdoings as well as the hurts and

---

[6] Bevans and Schroeder, *Constants in Context*, 10.

wounds born from others' actions, emotional as well physical. Both of these human dynamics—admitting failure and sin and seeking forgiveness, and forgiving another's sin—shape human life, families as well as societies, in multiple ways. How disciples respond as both sinner and sinned-against determines to a large extent the quality of their lives as well as the testimony it bears. If disciples fail to make amends for the wrongs committed, they can become self-righteous or self-justifying, believing there is no need to seek forgiveness, or they can hide in fear, shame, and guilt, paralyzing and binding life into a kind of death. And when disciples are hurt by others, if they do not, in time, work toward forgiving, they risk living in anger, bitterness, and revenge, eventually seeking an eye for an eye. Disciples can also make excuses for the other's wrongdoing and not hold them accountable, leaving themselves open to being a doormat that others can step all over. None of these conditions is a particularly appealing way to live and is not what following Jesus is all about. Being called into the fellowship of Christ with other disciples means learning to become a forgiver, to reconcile grievances with our neighbor, which involves both the practice of forgiving those who sin against us and seeking forgiveness from those we sin against. In the great dance of forgiveness, disciples seek and receive God's forgiveness.

In the Hebrew Bible, forgiveness is associated with a number of ideas: "wiping away," "sending away," "removing," and "covering." The Israelites came to understand over the course of their relationship with Yahweh that their sins separated them from the divine covenant but that the covenant could be restored through repentance, atonement, and seeking Yahweh's forgiveness. Seeking reconciliation in the context of the Hebraic covenant means restoring relationships to their rightful place, both with God and with neighbor. The Israelite community developed rituals of atonement and sacrifice through burnt offerings that expressed the destruction of their sin. Animal sacrifice symbolized a "guilt offering" through which sins are confessed and the priest declares, "you shall be forgiven" (Lev 5:10ff). In addition to rituals, the community's leaders pleaded with God in prayer to forgive the people's sins and restore the bonds of the covenant. Moses prayed, "Forgive the iniquity of this people according to the greatness of your steadfast love" (Num 14:19), and Solomon implored God to "Hear the plea of your servant and of your people Israel when they pray towards this place; O hear in heaven your dwelling place; heed and forgive" (1 Kgs 8:30).

The authors of the Hebrew Bible texts were not afraid to reveal the reality of unforgiveness, the struggle to forgive and the desire at times to not forgive. The psalmist is well known for hurling bitterness toward his or her enemies and the enemies of God: "O that you would kill the wicked, O God!" (Ps 139:19). The prophets also tell God *not* to forgive the sinner. Isaiah says, "And so people are humbled, and everyone is brought low—do not forgive them!" (Isa 2:9). Jeremiah repeats a similar refrain, "Do not forgive their iniquity, do not blot out their sin from your sight" (Jer 18:23). But in that struggle to understand divine forgiveness, the prophets also proclaim God's perspective on forgiveness: "I will cleanse them from all the guilt of their sin against me, and I will forgive all the guilt of their sin and rebellion against me" (Jer 33:8). What disciples of Yahweh must learn is that God's forgiveness does not make sense (Isa 55:8): a follower can never gain forgiveness or equality with God by an act of reparation or ritual sacrifice. "For you have no delight in sacrifice; if I were to give a burnt offering, you would not be pleased" (Ps 51:16). Rather a "broken and contrite heart" is the sign that the follower knows his or her sin and lack of love and seeks to be in communion with Yahweh again. The prophets too had to learn that God forgives because God loves: "I will love them freely, for my anger has turned from them" (Hos 14:4).

An essential claim to Christian faith is that no person on his or her own can relieve him- or herself of the burden of sin or muster what is needed to forgive the wrongs they endure. Forgiving neighbors and asking forgiveness is not a matter of human accomplishment, greater personal effort, or heroism. The practice of forgiveness is grounded in the recognition that God's love conquers all sin, a love that empowers disciples to seek and grant forgiveness in the face of much pain and hurt. Neighbor love precedes neighbor forgiveness in the Christian story. Joseph's brothers realize when their father is dead that Joseph will not only hold a grudge against them but pay them back in full. They go to ask forgiveness: "please forgive the crime of the servants of the God of your father" and they do so "as your slaves" (Gen 50:17ff), never imagining that Joseph will accept them as brothers. Joseph weeps upon hearing their request for forgiveness and embraces them, not as slaves, but as brothers, promising that "I myself will provide for you and your little ones." Joseph models the practice of love through forgiving those who sinned against him.

This is the model Jesus follows and teaches: because Yahweh loves, Yahweh forgives, but this forgiveness comes when sinners seek forgiveness from one another, thereby restoring a community of love. In fact, for Jesus, divine and human reconciliation are caught up with each other: without forgiving a neighbor a wrong, God will not forgive our wrongs, and without seeking God's forgiveness for our sins, we have little capacity to become forgivers. "For if you forgive others their trespasses, your heavenly Father will also forgive you; but if you do not forgive others, neither will your Father forgive your trespasses" (Matt 6:14-15).

Central to Jesus' witness about God is the radical, abundant, merciful love that God offers. Forgiveness is God's very nature and mission, because God is divine communion that is self-giving love. God is forgiveness who empowers Jesus to practice divine forgiveness and extend the power to forgive sins to his followers. Forgiveness is not a hardship for God, as the Israelites learned over time, and God does not respond in anger or retribution, but embraces all sinners who return with a humble heart. Reconciliation is at the heart of divine mission.

Jesus preaches this radical gospel of divine love and forgiveness, and heals sinners who are estranged from God and community. Jesus comes on the heels of John the Baptist announcing the forgiveness of sins (Mark 1:4; Luke 1:77; 3:3). A paralyzed man receives both healing and forgiveness (Matt 9:2ff), and the woman who anoints Jesus' feet pours out love that flows from the forgiveness she has experienced (Luke 7:47). To those who do not observe the ritual law, to the outcast and the sick, to those who have done wrong, Jesus proclaims, "Friend, your sins are forgiven you" (Luke 5:20).

Not always good news, however. Some could not accept this view of divine forgiveness, or Jesus' claim that he forgives sinners. Jesus tries to make the teaching on forgiveness easier to practice: "Do not judge, and you will not be judged; do not condemn, and you will not be condemned. Forgive, and you will be forgiven" (Luke 6:37). Yet even that teaching is rejected. Charges of blasphemy against Jesus are closely tied to his proclamation of forgiveness of sins (Luke 5:21). His own suffering and execution, as an innocent person in the face of false charges, brings Jesus to a place of abandonment, loneliness, and pain. And yet, Jesus' love for God and his followers led him to a radical step of obedience, to lay down his life for his friends and to offer forgiveness to those who crucify him. In Luke's gospel, Jesus is the ultimate reconciler, offering healing and hope to the guilty criminal being crucified alongside him at the same time that he begs God to forgive those who wronged him (Luke 23:32-43). Jesus bears a forgiveness born out of neighbor love and compassion, even for those who reject, betray, judge, and condemn him.

But forgiveness in practice is a difficult path to follow, both in seeking forgiveness and in granting it. Many of the wounds people bear at the expense of violence, murder, war, torture, or rape are so horrible it takes years to find comfort, healing, and reconciliation. Because disciples understand their call as members of the Body of Christ, it seems hard to accept that the very relationships that are meant to give life and companionship are oftentimes the source of our greatest pain and suffering. Forgiveness is not a simple matter in human relationships. Most often, it is a process that takes time, healing, and the help of others. Those who suffer innocently need time to gain perspective on painful situations, face difficult emotions, and search for strength and courage—facets of human experience that can easily be ignored or repressed. Methodist theologian Gregory Jones calls the process the "dance of forgiveness" by which he means the movements that must be learned to live a way of forgiveness. He reminds us that forgiveness begins in witness: telling the truth about what has happened and identifying the anger, hurt, and pain experienced. From this pain comes a desire to live beyond it, not necessarily forgetting or dismissing it, but living differently in relationship to the hurt. Forgiveness also invites a disciple to see the wrongdoer as God sees them, as a child of God who needs healing and forgiveness. It may be difficult to initially grasp this view of a wrongdoer, but disciples take the first step when they utter the prayer of Jesus, "Father, forgive them" (Luke 23:34). In other words, disciples are invited by Christ to see sinners as neighbors.

When disciples face their own sinful acts, the steps of the dance apply as well. For the sinner, the steps to forgiveness begin with contrition, the heartfelt sense that I have committed a wrong and must seek to restore the broken relationship with my neighbor and with God. Contrition is the desire to be free from the burden of sin and guilt. I must be able to confess my sin, to give a witness to the truth of what I have done, and to acknowledge that the person I have harmed is a child of God. I repent the sin: admitting I was wrong. I can also give witness to the reality of God's all-embracing love that has forgiven and healed me in the past. In seeking God's forgiveness disciples are renewed to take up the life of discipleship again, which entails a commitment to change. From this broader vision of God's loving mercy in relationship to the sinner and the victim can come a commitment to change the circumstances that lead to such brokenness. Forgiveness is the path that leads to reconciliation, a commitment to change.

To be forgiven by God demands that the Christian become a forgiver: to offer forgiveness to others when sinned against, to accept the forgiveness of others, and to offer healing and consolation when there is pain and misery. As Jones says, forgiveness is not an isolated act or feeling, but a way of life that is "shaped by an ever-deepening friendship with

God and other people" that aims toward restoring communion.[7] Being a forgiver involves a lifetime of learning, because forgiveness means not just forgiving "seven times" but "seventy-seven times" (Matt 18:21-22).

Prophet

To be a neighbor is also to be a prophet. Prophets are a witness with a keen perception for what harms a neighbor: scorn, hatred, disobedience, hubris, unbelief, greed, and selfishness. Prophets see a larger reality within the neighborhood: they give witness to neighbor relations that become distorted, forgotten, and abused. A prophet can see social and cultural realities that harm people's lives on a personal, interpersonal, and systemic level. Disciples are called to embrace their call to be a prophet when they witness harm, evil, or oppression that besets a neighbor. Disciples are prophets when they demand that neighbors not be harmed by either individuals or systems, when they call the community back to its covenant with God, and when they work to change patterns of wickedness that destroy human life and flourishing. Prophets are witnesses to the power of the Spirit in transforming human hearts and minds. As Bevans notes, "The church's mission is about cooperating with God in the call of all people always and everywhere, to justice, peace and the integrity of the creation."[8]

In Hebrew *nabi* means "one called" or "one who is called" to speak, not his or her own words, but to speak God's words. In this sense, prophets are witnesses of God's justice. The later prophets, or writing prophets, were clearly called to exhort the people to renounce the popular though false actions and values they had adopted, and return to the life of the covenant. Being called upon to be a prophet was surely not wanted (Amos 7:14-15) or deeply admired by the people. Prophets are sent to their neighbors with a message about the state of human dignity and the dire prospects of the common good. Each prophet directed his message to a particular people undergoing a particular hardship, yet each focused on the need for diligent faith in the face of hardship, repentance for how neighbors were being treated, especially the poor and vulnerable, warnings of Yahweh's wrath and judgment if change did not come about, and hope in returning to God's covenant and favor (Isa 9:1-6;

---

[7] Gregory L. Jones, "Forgiveness," in *Practicing Our Faith: A Way of Life for a Searching People*, ed. Dorothy C. Bass (San Francisco, CA: Jossey-Bass, 1997), 134.

[8] Bevans and Schroeder, *Constants in Context*, 369.

11:1-9; Mic 6:8; 7:8-20; Jer 31:31-34). Hosea, a prophet of divine compassion (Hos 11:8-9), reminds the people that God's covenant is not just a legal agreement, but born of a deep love for the people, a personal relationship between Yahweh and the people. He reminds the people that even though God punishes their stubborn ways, Yahweh is always ready to forgive and welcome them back.

Prophets arise in Israel and are active during political and religious crises. Prophets preached repentance and reform during the Assyrian invasions and occupations (Amos, Hosea, First Isaiah, Micah), the decline of Judah and the Babylonian exile (Jeremiah, Ezekiel, Second Isaiah), and the postexilic period (Third Isaiah, Zechariah). Each in their own way look to Israel's history as one of unbroken faithfulness by Yahweh and continual unfaithfulness by the people. This dynamic helps to explain what has happened over the course of history as Israel moves from being a great and mighty nation to one dominated and oppressed by outside forces. Obedience easily turns to disobedience and true worship becomes a mockery as idols and foreign gods were praised and trusted over Yahweh. Prophets are particularly sensitive to practices of false worship and false testimony (Isa 1:13; Mic 7:7).

Jesus is also regarded as a prophet, a teacher, and preacher who is part of the prophetic tradition. In Luke's gospel he begins his ministry by reading from the prophet Isaiah (Luke 4:18-19). Many recognize him as a prophet (Mark 6:15; 8:27-29), an identity and ministry he shares with his cousin, John the Baptist. Like prophets before him, Jesus calls people to repentance, invites them into a relationship with a loving and merciful God, and warns them against false religious practices and injustice toward the poor and outcast. Unlike Israel's prophets, however, Jesus does not attempt to interpret the history of the covenant and the decline of the nation. Rather he is announcing "good news" about God's presence in the midst of the people now, a presence he seems to know and experience and that emanates from him as something radically new and different.

Jesus' preaching challenged prevailing conceptions about the course of history. While many awaited the coming of the Messiah, the Jewish community expressed a variety of attitudes about what God would do: some preached an apocalyptic end; the Essenes withdrew to create a separate, holy community; zealots sought a revolution; and the temple priests continued to seek God through ritual sacrifice. Jesus chose none of these routes, but rather preached the reign of God, not as a place or a new phase of Israel's nationhood, but a profound way of encountering

God in the present and future times by a new set of relationships. The reign of God, he teaches, is the power of God active in history that liberates the oppressed, saves the lost, forgives the sinner, mends the brokenhearted, heals the sick, and offers new life to the dying. The kingdom Jesus preaches is in continuity with the covenant tradition, but in ways that shocked and upset many of his listeners. Jesus' prophetic message is that God's love and mercy extends to all regardless of their sin, status, or ritual purity. In other words, no barrier stands in the way of God's love and justice to people. Jesus' healings also point to God's radical power to overcome all forms of evil and suffering, to restore all brokenness to wholeness, the sick to health, and the dead to resurrection. Jesus claims that God's work is taking place now, it is "at hand" and can be known and experienced. But it is also "not yet," something to come in the future, which will be like a great wedding banquet, including many neighbors most people would *not* want to be invited (Matt 22:1-14; Luke 14:16-24).

Jesus' message disappoints and infuriates listeners, both because they want another kind of kingdom but also because he is making claims about God and his relationship with God that are deemed blasphemous. Jesus is forsaken and rejected, crucified and killed, because of his prophetic stance. After Jesus' resurrection, prophecy became one of the gifts of the Spirit and at least in some congregations was a regular part of worship (1 Thess 5:20; 1 Cor 12:28-29; 14:26-32).

In following Jesus as prophet, a disciple grows into a profound sense of each aspect of discipleship: the cost of following, the practice of true worship, the struggle to see others as neighbor, the dance of forgiveness, and the practice of stewardship. With a view to the whole of discipleship, a disciple can claim a prophetic voice in the community, calling fellow members to the fullness of life in Christ. As Jesus shows, prophets do not change much in people if they only condemn their faults; a prophet seems to have a better chance if they announce the good news about God's mission.

Stewards

Being a steward, and practicing stewardship, derives from being creatures of a created world. God creates and is the first steward of creation, extending the responsibility for stewardship to humanity. Because God is the source of all that is and because God claims creation to be "good," disciples live in the world for the sake of the world with a spirit of gratitude, humility, and awe (Gen 1:31). Each human person is created as *imago Dei* (Gen 1:27), as "partakers of the divine nature" (2 Pet 1:3), and this radical identity includes responsibility for filling the earth and practicing dominion over all living things (Gen 1:28). The psalmist notes the amazing juxtaposition between humanity's smallness in comparison to their immense calling and responsibility: "What are human beings that you are mindful of them, mortals that you care for them? Yet you have made them a little lower than God, and crowned them with glory and honor," sharing in God's stewardship over all creation (Ps 8:3-8).

Dominion means disciples pursue a proper relationship to the whole order of creation, to keep and till, to serve, preserve, and cultivate the gifts of the earth (Gen 2:15). Stewards have dominion over the earth in order to be its guardians, custodians, and preservers. The authors of the Genesis story identify humanity's connection to the earth through two important names: "Adam," which in Hebrew (*Adama*) means of the earth, topsoil, or ground, one who comes from the dust and the earth and returns there; and "Eve" (*Hava*), meaning "living," the mother of all living things (Gen 3:20). Together humanity's parents are *Adama* and *Hava*, soil and life.

Through this connection to the earth and all living things, the biblical understanding of a steward develops in relationship to the person who has responsibility for the goods of the household, including food, property, money, and land. A steward, in the Greek Hebrew Bible, is called *oikonomos*, which combines the terms "house" and "to manage" (*oikos + nemein*), a term drawn from common ancient Greek usage. A steward serves his or her master by overseeing the master's table, property, and finances. The sustenance of the family household depends on proper stewardship to thrive (Gen 43:19, 24; 44:1-4).

Stewardship is a dimension of the covenant and is directly related to the community's care for its neighbors as well as its religious rituals and laws, all of which serve to express thanksgiving and praise to and for its divine source. In the Hebrew Bible the covenant requires that members care for the material needs of impoverished family members (Lev 25:35-43), celebrate sabbatical and jubilee years (Lev 25:1-17), offer first fruits (Deut 18:3-5; 26:1-2), tithe (Gen 14:20; 28:22; Mal 3:8; Neh 10:37), offer hospitality to the stranger (Gen 18:1-15), and remember and observe the Sabbath (Exod 20:8-11). In a variety of ways, then, the covenant entails the practice of stewardship through concern for the poor, sharing of personal resources, and recognition of the true source of life and sustenance.

But even good stewards can be tempted by riches, the false promises of other gods, and prosperity. Moses, who God "entrusted with all my house" (Num 12:7; Heb 3:1), tells the Israelites time and again to remember their liberation from slavery and all that God has done for them (Deut 8:1-6) and will do for them when the Lord God brings the community "into a good land, a land with flowing streams, with springs and underground waters" (Deut 8:7-10).

Jesus is called the good shepherd (John 10:11), but he could easily, like Moses, be called the good steward. He shares the same stewardship over God's house and people as its servant, as steward of all God's gifts. Jesus is God's gift to the world, and he extends himself as a gift to everyone he encounters. He stewards the vocation he has been called to, faithfully fulfilling his call to serve and to die, completely emptying himself in obedient love (Phil 2:6).

Jesus also uses the image of the steward to demonstrate generosity, wisdom, and prudence (Matt 24:45-51; 25:14-30), as well as shrewdness (Luke 16:1-9). The disciple is like a good steward, a person who is given great responsibility but who can easily be tempted by power and authority. Whether it is great material wealth or authority over land, slaves, or armies, Jesus links faithful stewardship to discipleship. "From everyone to whom much has been given, much will be required; and from the one to whom much has been entrusted, even more will be demanded" (Luke 12:48). In this sense, disciples are stewards of the goods of creation and the goods that society produces and uses; they watch over and care for the resources of the Christian community, including its organizational structures, processes, material goods, and financial resources. Stewardship is essential to mission.

St. Paul uses the idea of steward in relationship to the faith that has been given to the community. Paul reminds the Corinthians that disciples are "servants of Christ and stewards of God's mysteries" (1 Cor 4:1). Disciples are stewards of all that is necessary to carry forth the church's mission, including the Scriptures and tradition that bear the truth to which they give witness. For Paul the church is the "household of faith" (Gal 6:10), and the "economy of God" pertains to the way God cares for the whole household of the universe from creation to the final coming. Disciples are made in the image of God through Christ (Col 1:15; 2 Cor 4:4), and all things are brought to perfection in and through Christ (Eph 1:9).

Paul identifies himself as a servant in God's plan of salvation (Col 1:25), one who is commissioned by grace to bear the message of salvation (Eph 3:2). Within the "economy of salvation," the whole church becomes a witness, a servant, and a steward of the great mysteries of faith. In

Colossians 1:25 the author links *diakonia* and *oikonomia*: "I became [the church's] servant [*diakonos*] according to God's commission [*oikonomian tou theou*] that was given to me for you, to make the word of God fully known, the mystery that has been hidden throughout the ages and generations but has now been revealed to his saints." Early Christian authors of Ephesians and Colossians emphasized the idea of the economy of God's plan for all creation that is now fully revealed in Christ, which comes to full expression in the patristic idea that everything is "from the Father, through the Son, in the Holy Spirit."[9]

Finally, disciples are stewards of a vocation, the gifts received for service in the community. Like Paul, disciples must become stewards of these gifts: "Like good stewards of the manifold grace of God, serve one another with whatever gift each of you has received" (1 Pet 4:10).

In this chapter I have examined seven features of discipleship. There are no doubt many other ways of naming and analyzing the life and practice of Christian discipleship. In some ways discipleship cannot be fully defined and grasped. It is not a program to be implemented or something we can set out to achieve. It is an identity, a commitment, a way of life, and a response to a call. In naming these features I have attempted to identify the particular parameters and markers of discipleship as I understand them in the New Testament. To be a disciple means to be a follower of Christ, committed to learning his ways; to be a worshiper, joining Christ and the community in praise of God's wonders; to be a witness who proclaims the good news to the world; to be a neighbor by living mindfully of others' needs and reaching out to them with compassion; to be a forgiver by practicing reconciliation, healing, and peacemaking; to be a prophet willing to tell the truth about the injustices that harm neighbors; and to be stewards of the creation, the community, and the mysteries of the faith. Disciples are able to take up and imitate the way of Christ because Jesus embodies first and foremost the way of being a follower, worshiper, witness, forgiver, neighbor, prophet, and steward.

In Jesus, we experience the divine life drawing near in a human person. By the power of the Spirit, his followers continued the practices of discipleship that he taught them, taking up a life in community that gives witness to his life, death, and resurrection. Hence the church is born of water and blood, death and new life, Jesus and the Spirit. The same Spirit that empowered the first followers continues to grace Christians today

---

[9] LaCugna, *God for Us*, 25.

in the path of discipleship. We turn now to consider the ways in which the Spirit is present in the life of Jesus' followers.

Sources for Further Reading

Bass, Dorothy C., ed. *Practicing Our Faith: A Way of Life for a Searching People*. San Francisco, CA: Jossey-Bass, 1997.

Best, Ernest. *Disciples and Discipleship: Studies in the Gospel According to Mark*. Edinburgh: T&T Clark, 1986.

Bevans, Stephen B., and Roger P. Schroeder. *Constants in Context: A Theology of Mission for Today*. Maryknoll, NY: Orbis Books, 2004.

Brueggemann, Walter, and Patrick Miller. *The Word that Describes the World: The Bible and Discipleship*. Minneapolis, MN: Fortress Press, 2006.

Donahue, John R. *The Theology and Setting of Discipleship in the Gospel of Mark*. Milwaukee, WI: Marquette University Press, 1983.

Fitzmyer, Joseph A. *Luke the Theologian: Aspects of his Teaching*. Mahwah, NJ: Paulist Press, 1989.

Long, Thomas G. *Testimony: Talking Ourselves into Being Christian*. San Francisco, CA: Jossey-Bass, 2004.

Longenecker, Richard N., ed. *Patterns of Discipleship in the New Testament*. Grand Rapids, MI: Wm. B. Eerdmans, 1996.

O'Grady, John F. *Disciples and Leaders: The Origins of Christian Ministry in the New Testament*. New York: Paulist Press, 1991.

Segovia, Fernando F. *Discipleship in the New Testament*. Philadelphia, PA: Fortress Press, 1985.

Tilley, Terrance W. *The Disciples' Jesus: Christology as Reconciling Practice*. Maryknoll, NY: Orbis Books, 2008.

Chapter 2

Gifts for Service: Charisms and Vocation in the Christian Life

Discipleship is initiated in the waters of baptism by the power of the Spirit in the community of disciples. From its beginnings, discipleship is a sacramental reality bearing the symbols of a new identity in a new community through blessing, water, fire, anointing, and proclamation. As Mark Searle notes, baptism is an initiation into a journey "back to God from whom one came." Disciples begin a way of life that is "following in the footsteps of Christ in the company of his disciples."[1]

In the waters of baptism an initiate undergoes a fundamental reorientation of their life and identity. To be baptized in water signifies the destruction of sin, the giving up of the "old life," and the purification and regeneration of a "new life" in Christ. As Paul notes, "So if anyone is in Christ, there is a new creation: everything old has passed away; see, everything has become new! All this is from God" (2 Cor 5:17). Baptism is a drowning in darkness and death, according to Tertullian, and an emergence into light and life. The ritual of baptism marks the way of life for disciples. As Richard Fragomeni notes, we "live in a baptismal mode," we are always being baptized into the dynamic movement between death and life, sin and reconciliation, evil and justice, the old and the new (Rom 6:1-11; Col 2:12-13).[2]

---

[1] Mark Searle, *Christening: The Making of Christians* (Collegeville, MN: Liturgical Press, 1980), 1.

[2] Richard N. Fragomeni, *Come to the Light: An Invitation to Baptism and Confirmation* (New York: Continuum, 1999), 28–29.

In addition to baptism in water, disciples are baptized in the Spirit, into a divine reality that is at once incarnational and eschatological. As Jesus proclaims, "Very truly, I tell you, no one can enter the kingdom of God without being born of water and Spirit" (John 3:5). Through water and the Spirit, Christian baptism is a rebirth into the *imago Christi* (Matt 3:11-12; Mark 1:7-8; Luke 3:15-18), taking on Christ's likeness in order to take up Christ's mission. "We are Christened in baptism. Baptism makes us another Christ."[3] In the baptismal liturgy and again in the Holy Saturday liturgy, Christians are asked to respond and make a promise: to renounce evil and commit to live a new life in Christ. This promise is what Fragomeni calls the "vow to be Christ." "We vow to surrender ourselves and our own identities to a Christlikeness . . . to make an unconditional commitment of availability to God and one another. . . . We vow to be Christ for all people in their need and in their pain and to be available, inclusively, to all. We vow to be of service to all for the freedom of all from the bias and bondage of sin. We vow this Christlikeness."[4]

Rising out of the baptismal waters, disciples are anointed in baptism and confirmation *into* the Anointed One, the Body of Christ, as priest, prophet, and king. This claim echoes that of Cyril of Jerusalem: "As partakers of Christ, therefore, you are rightly called 'Christs,' 'anointed ones.' You became Christs by receiving the . . . Holy Spirit: everything has been wrought in you 'likewise' because you are likenesses of Christ."[5] Christians share in Christ's priesthood through living a life of worship, adoration, and sacrifice; in his call as prophet in giving witness to neighbor love, mercy, and justice; and in the kingly role through service and stewardship of God's community and creation.

Baptism, then, reorients and defines Christian identity in at least three ways. First, baptism is personal insofar as God claims each person to be a beloved child, created by God and called by name to live the way of Jesus Christ through the power of the Holy Spirit. To name a child is a tremendous responsibility for parents because a name becomes forged with an identity for a lifetime. Joseph names Mary's son "Jesus" in Matthew's

[3] Ibid., 59.

[4] Ibid., 52–53.

[5] "The Holy Chrism," Third Lecture on the Mysteries, in *The Works of Saint Cyril of Jerusalem*, vol. 2, trans. Leo P. McCauley and Anthony A. Stephenson, The Fathers of the Church Series, vol. 64 (Washington, DC: The Catholic University of America, 1970), 168–69.

gospel, a name derived from Josiah, which means "God saves." So deeply is Jesus' identity tied to his name, that the New Testament writer's identify Jesus of Nazareth with many names, probably because no single name captures completely who and what he is. In the birth narratives, he is named the Christ, Messiah, Son of Man, Son of God, Emmanuel, Savior, Son of Abraham, Son of David, and Lord (Matt 1:1-25; Luke 2:10-11). All these names cast some insight into the mystery of who Jesus is. A child's naming at baptism signifies a new identity in Christ in his community, a name commonly referred to as our Christian name.

Second, baptism is communal and social. It is the church that baptizes (Acts 2:37-41). The community stands as witness to a new life in Christ and promises that the way of discipleship will be made known to initiates. Baptism incorporates a person into the Body of Christ, a community that shares the call to discipleship. Theologians remind us that persons are social beings: we come to be we who are in and through relationship. Discipleship constitutes a new way of "social being" for now all relationships are defined in and through Christian discipleship. The church, as a community of disciples, shares in a life together for the sake of the world.

For Paul it was imperative that the communities he founded understand that this ecclesial and communal identity is fundamental to life in Christ. He reminds his readers over and over that by virtue of baptism in Christ they are unified in the one Spirit, "Jew or Greeks, slaves or free" (1 Cor 12:13). This ecclesial identity creates the unity of one Body in which no person is more or less than another, "for in Christ Jesus you are all children of God through faith. As many of you as were baptized into Christ have clothed yourselves with Christ" (Gal 3:26-27). And this unity, this community, finds its origin in the oneness of God: "There is one body and one Spirit, just as you were called to the one hope of your calling, one Lord, one faith, one baptism, one God and Father of all, who is above all and through all and in all" (Eph 4:4-6).

A third way in which baptism reorients a person is through a sense of call. Baptism is vocational. The washing and anointing, the casting off of the old and the embrace of the new, symbolize the Christian's identity as one who is called to a particular way of life. God's radical free offer of loving redemption is proclaimed in baptism. God's extended hand draws the initiate out of the waters, God calls by name, God commands to leave everything behind and become a follower in the way of Christ. Baptism initiates us into the way of discipleship, a journey that demands the whole self for one's whole life. Our fundamental call is to be a disciple by living the way of discipleship.

Discipleship is the shared communal calling to a life of service for the sake of God's world. Through the waters of baptism, Christians together heed God's call and promise to embrace a common way of life—a life of discipleship in communion for mission. This is the most basic, elemental, and foundational reality, identity, and promise of the Christian. It is what constitutes a people, a holy people, the people of God.

Call and Vocation

The call to discipleship is a personal, communal, and vocational reality. As Scripture demonstrates, to be called by Yahweh is a deeply personal reality with profound communal implications. Yahweh calls people to repent their sins, follow a new path, take a new name, and embrace a new relationship. Likewise, the community experiences a profound call from slavery into a new identity, a new people. In each instance, God initiates a call and invites a response, one that is both loving and kind as well as relentlessly demanding. Absent trust in Yahweh's call, the stories also reveal what we know to be true of our own lives: time and again we go astray and do not heed the call. After he is called by name at baptism, Jesus immediately takes up the task of calling others to repentance and to follow after him in a new way of life. Jesus' mission to preach the good news, to forgive sinners, and heal the sick, draws all who will follow after him into a new relationship with "Abba, Father." In this way Jesus takes up God's mission to reach out to all people and call them into the path of discipleship.

The word "vocation" comes from the Latin word, *vocare*, which means "to call." In the Latin West the idea of vocation has a long and interesting history. In the Catholic context it traditionally referred to a divine calling to a particular state of life, that of priesthood or religious life in a monastery or convent, which corresponded with living a celibate life. Within this context, vocation rarely referred to work or marriage and family. In the sixteenth century Protestant reformers rejected the notion that only priests, monks, and nuns have a vocation, or that any vocation is higher than another. Martin Luther's teaching on the priesthood of all believers emphasizes that each Christian has a vocation, a calling, by virtue of their standing or office in the world. It is through faith, for Luther, that one accepts one's divinely appointed standing and lives out that faith through the good works of daily life, whether as a cobbler, painter, spouse, or son. Each of these paths gives glory to God. As revolutionary as his perspective was at the time, Luther has been criticized for a static view of vocation, the idea that God sets down each person's place in the world, which must be accepted and carried out. But Luther was also able to see that vocation implies relationship and service to others in all parts of life; it is personal, ecclesial, what Luther calls a "spiritual calling," as well as social, an "external calling" in the world. The call to Christian love and service is expressed precisely in and through relationships, family, and work.[6]

Today many Protestant and Catholic theologians have moved beyond narrow views of vocation to embrace the idea that vocation first and foremost addresses God's call to the whole person in relationship to their whole life. In other words, vocation is not reserved for only a select group of people, a particular lifestyle, or to some forms of work and profession. I understand the category of vocation in both a broad and specific way. Broadly speaking, all Christians have a common vocation to discipleship, a shared calling. But vocation is also specific. It refers to the particularity of our callings, the way each person is summoned by God to live faithfully given their talents, gifts, and circumstances.

Taking human life as a whole, I define Christian vocation as *the response to God's call and the Spirit's charisms manifest in adult life commitments in relationship to three aspects of the self: (1) how I live, particularly in relationship to permanent postbaptism commitments; (2) what I do, the service I offer to God in and for a community; and (3) who I am, the sense of self as it relates to my personal, historical, cultural, and social contexts.[7] Our baptismal identity and call to be a Christian disciple is lived out in and through the particular callings that constitute our vocation.* In the rest of the chapter I will explore each of these claims: vocation is a category that generally refers to a way of life forged in adulthood; the idea of gifts, particularly those of charisms that become the pneumatological foundation of vocation; how charisms

---

[6] Douglas J. Schuurman, *Vocation: Discerning Our Callings in Life* (Grand Rapids, MI: Wm. B. Eerdmans, 2004), 4–8. For a discussion of vocation in the Reformation, with excerpts from original writings, see William C. Placher, ed. *Callings: Twenty Centuries of Christian Wisdom on Vocation* (Grand Rapids, MI: Wm. B. Eerdmans, 2005), 205–38.

[7] I am drawing from the work of Marie Theresa Coombs and Francis Kelly Nemeck, OMI, who define vocation as constituting three interrelated aspects of personhood in adult life: *who* the Lord calls us *to be* (our self-identity); *how* the Lord calls us *to become* our unique selves in God (our vocational lifestyle); and *what* the Lord calls us *to do* for God and for others (our mission or ministry). Marie Theresa Coombs and Francis Kelly Nemeck, *Discerning Vocations to Marriage, Celibacy and Singlehood* (Collegeville, MN: Liturgical Press, 1994), 2–5.

are manifest in life commitments such as marriage, celibacy, and single life, and work, labor, and service; and our sense of self in time, culture, and history.

Vocation Emerges in Adulthood

In many ways, claiming that vocation is an adult reality is not new, since the idea of calling to priesthood or one's standing in life implied the call of an adult Christian. More precisely, I am claiming that the call to discipleship, not vocation, is the primary reality for children and teens. Learning what it means to be a disciple constitutes one of the main focuses of early faith development, something that is never complete at a certain point in life. Learning is a lifetime commitment for the disciple. Vocation may begin to emerge in the early years, but it evolves as a person matures and responds to God's call over the course of life. We discern gifts *toward* vocation in children and youth; we recognize their interests, affirm their gifts and talents, and encourage them to explore new interests. Charisms are beginning to emerge and are formed, and sometimes malformed, under varying familial, social, educational, religious, and cultural conditions. Youth and young adults need people who recognize their gifts and can mentor them through a variety of experiences in order that they can see how their gifts might be offered in meaningful work and relationships. Young people need ample opportunities to "test" their gifts by trying on different roles in various contexts. Such experiences are crucial for testing charisms that are the basis of vocation. In essence, call and gifts for discipleship are present from baptism till death; vocations emerge, are discerned over time, and can change during the course of a lifetime.

Does this mean that God predetermines or sets down a vocation that must be discerned and figured out by each person? Because vocation is a calling that encompasses our whole life, both temporal and eternal, as Marie Theresa Coombs and Francis Kelly Nemeck point out, "the Lord wills us to be transformed in God, wills us to become our transformed selves through a certain lifestyle and wills us to accomplish some mission."[8] I agree with the authors that God's calling is not specific, predetermined, or absolute insofar as "the Lord is free to call in a specific way

[8] Ibid., 20.

or in a general way." Whatever way in which God calls, the "ultimate realization" of vocation is "transformation in God, by God—our personal deification," a call to radical holiness.[9] Vocation is the specific way in which discipleship is lived, transforming persons into their Christlikeness.

Vocation is complex and multifaceted and is not determined once and for all in a person's life. Rather, it is a dynamic response through a variety of choices that can change over time due to various personal and social contexts and how the Spirit is active and interactive in these contexts. God calls us and God responds to our responses to that call: if we say yes, God invites us to live more fully and deeply in our calling; if we say no, God continues to convert our hearts; and if we say maybe, God is patient and accompanies us toward decision.[10] In Coombs and Nemeck's theology of vocation, we are in an intimate dance and dialogue with God throughout our lives about how to live out God's purpose for us, which ultimately is to move more deeply into relationship with the divine presence.

What is the relationship between who I am, how I live my commitments, and what I do? Do we have one vocation that includes three different facets, or multiple vocations that must be reconciled into one? The challenge of integrating these three aspects into one life, a unity of who I am, how I live, and what I do, is certainly the challenge of adult life as we know it today. It is finding what Paul calls "our way of life" for which "God made us" (Eph 2:10).

Irrevocable Gifts and Charisms

For Paul, God has made known this way of life through Christ in the power of the Spirit. But what, in Paul's terms, distinguishes the call to the shared life of discipleship and the particular and unique call termed "vocation"? One answer can be found in his understanding of grace and charisms. The Greek word for "grace" is *charis*, meaning a free gift that brings delight, joy, love, gratitude, pleasure, and kindness.[11] Christians have long emphasized the total free gifting of divine grace, a gift not granted because of merit or reward, but because of God's sheer love. As Paul exclaims, "For by grace you have been saved through faith, and

---

[9] Ibid., 1.

[10] Ibid., 26.

[11] Harley H. Schmitt, *Many Gifts, One Lord* (Minneapolis, MN: Augsburg, 1993), 16ff.

this is not your own doing; it is the gift of God—not the result of works, so that no one may boast" (Eph 2:8-9; see also, Rom 5:15-16; 6:23). Grace is God's love in relationship, an enacted love, a love continually present calling forth our response. To say that God relates to creation and humanity "graciously" is to claim that grace is who God is and what God does in relationship. When Christians claim that we are "given" grace we recognize God as sharing God's self with us; grace is not a reality separate from who God is, but the human experience of God's overwhelming loving presence. In and through Christ we have experienced this grace anew, the one who is sheer gift of God, a gift "full of grace [*charis*] and truth" (John 1:14).

Paul distinguishes two kinds of grace-gifts. The first are universal gifts that all Christians receive, gifts of faith, hope, and charity. Paul reminds the Corinthians that charity is the most essential gift because it unifies all other gifts and lasts (1 Cor 12:27–13:1; Eph 4:15-16). Faith, hope, and charity have long been understood as divine gifts that enable the Christian to embrace and embody Christ's call to full relationship with God and neighbor. Without these fundamental gifts of the Spirit, discipleship remains a purely human effort. Faith, hope, and love are gifts that empower and unify the features of discipleship explained in the first chapter.

In addition to universal gifts, Paul recognizes that each person in the community receives special or unique gifts. Each person is capable of different kinds of service and he calls this second type of gift "charism." The Greek word *charismata* is a plural form of the noun *charisma*, which is generally translated as "gift." Many words are derived from the Greek root *char*: joy is *chara*, rejoicing is *chairo*, thanksgiving is *eucharista*, bestowing is *charizomai*. God's grace is *charis*, a sheer gift that is universal and bestowed on all, whereas *charismata* are particular gifts that flow from grace. The particular gifts express different services, but the Spirit is the essence of the gift. In receiving and accepting these gifts we experience a sense of joy (*chara*) and thanksgiving (*eucharista*) (Acts 8:39; Matt 13:44; Acts 16:34; John 20:20).[12] Paul advances the idea of charisms in three letters: Romans 12:3-8; First Corinthians 12:4-11; and Ephesians 4:11-16.

> For by the grace given to me I say to everyone among you not to think of yourself more highly than you ought to think, but to think with sober judgment, each according to the measure of faith that

[12] Ibid., 45, 48–49.

God has assigned. For as in one body we have many members, and not all the members have the same function, so we, who are many, are one body in Christ, and individually we are members one of another. We have gifts that differ according to the grace given to us: prophecy, in proportion to faith; ministry, in ministering; the teacher, in teaching; the exhorter, in exhortation; the giver, in generosity; the leader, in diligence; the compassionate, in cheerfulness. (Rom 12:3-8)

Now there are varieties of gifts, but the same Spirit; and there are varieties of services, but the same Lord; and there are varieties of activities, but it is the same God who activates all of them in everyone. To each is given the manifestation of the Spirit for the common good. To one is given through the Spirit the utterance of wisdom, and to another the utterance of knowledge according to the same Spirit, to another faith by the same Spirit, to another gifts of healing by the one Spirit, to another the working of miracles, to another prophecy, to another the discernment of spirits, to another various kinds of tongues, to another the interpretation of tongues. All these are activated by one and the same Spirit, who allots to each one individually just as the Spirit chooses. (1 Cor 12:4-11)

The gifts he gave were that some would be apostles, some prophets, some evangelists, some pastors and teachers, to equip the saints for the work of ministry, for building up the body of Christ, until all of us come to the unity of the faith and of the knowledge of the Son of God, to maturity, to the measure of the full stature of Christ. We must no longer be children, tossed to and fro and blown about by every wind of doctrine, by people's trickery, by their craftiness in deceitful scheming. But speaking the truth in love, we must grow up in every way into him who is the head, into Christ, from whom the whole body, joined and knitted together by every ligament with which it is equipped, as each part is working properly, promotes the body's growth in building itself up in love. (Eph 4:11-16)

In each case Paul argues that charisms are particular and unique gifts granted by the Spirit to each person for the purpose of building up the community. In each letter he lists a variety of gifts, not in order to create an exhaustive list, but to illustrate the gifts he witnesses in each community and to make a point about their diversity and unity.[13] Paul's teaching on charisms is connected to two key ideas: diverse gifts are

---

[13] Thomas F. O'Meara, *Theology of Ministry*, rev. ed. (Mahwah, NJ: Paulist Press, 1999), 200–207.

needed for the common good and the building up of the Body of Christ, and together these gifts unify the community into one Body (1 Cor 1:10; Eph 1:1-2; 4:4-6; Phil 1:27). These two ideas may at first seem contrary or paradoxical, but in fact for Paul they are interdependent (1 Cor 12:4-6; Rom 12:4-6).

Paul explains that the Spirit gives many diverse gifts to the community. All members receive some charisms; in other words, no Christian is charism-exempt (1 Pet 4:10). But there is no single person who receives all the gifts, nor does it seem that an individual receives only one charism. Each person is a unique combination of charisms, and no two people hold exactly the same constellation (1 Cor 7:7). Perhaps like the human genome, there is a basic shared structure and yet no two persons are alike. Each person is unique.

Charisms are fundamentally gifts for service; they are capacities or qualities that people express through activities, actions, speech, and what today is commonly referred to as practices (which I will discuss in chapter 4). In other words charisms are not private, internal qualities, meant for self-improvement. They are to be embodied actions, lived out and expressed in word and deed. Charisms are not solely about gifts for ecclesial leadership either, but gifts given to the entire Body for the common good of the Body, some of which pertain to community leadership (1 Cor 12:7). The Spirit works in such a way as to ensure that charisms are always present in the community, that gifts are distributed and, if discerned and responded to, will enable the community to flourish in its mission (1 Cor 12:11). Charisms express diversity within the community, a diversity that recognizes that the health of the Body and the fulfillment of the community's mission are dependent on the flourishing of many gifts (1 Cor 12:12-13). Diverse gifts-for-mission also unify the community into one Body. Charisms, then, are a divine unifying reality. Through the exercise of many charisms, the various "parts" of the Body contribute to the whole, because the Body cannot function well or optimally without each person actualizing the gifts they have to share. Charisms are a gift to be received, recognized, and acted upon, which means they can be ignored, rejected, and diminished, by either individuals or the community. In other words, the granting of charisms by the Spirit requires an acceptance and a fertile ground for growth by the individual and the community.

Paul did not give a detailed explanation to early Christians on just how charisms work. He believed in the power of the Spirit to accomplish God's work through the community's giftedness. He spelled out his teaching on charism in the context of a real pastoral problem: quarreling among those who claimed that some gifts are higher and better than other gifts. In the case of the Corinthians, he had to show that extraordinary gifts are important but what the community requires is recognition of all gifts, most of which are ordinary (1 Cor 14:1-12). Ranking gifts usually leads to rancor and division.

How does the idea of charism help to explain the call of vocation? Charism can be a confusing category associated with images of ecstatic behavior in the moment. Certainly gifts of charismatic expression such as speaking in tongues are a tremendous expression of the Spirit's presence in the moment, but it is not the only expression as Paul notes. Charisms can be seen as the way in which God calls us, through the Spirit's promptings, in the course of our adult lives to offer gifts for the good of the community. Charisms, then, are the pneumatological foundation of vocation and mission. Since it is not common to make the link between vocation and charisms, several questions must be answered: Are charisms momentary or long-lasting? Can charisms cease and new charisms emerge? Are charisms automatic, granted in a state of perfection or wholeness, or do they exist as a possibility? How are charisms related to natural talents? Do charisms require effort and skill? Do we receive charisms for commitments such as marriage or celibate religious life, or are they primarily expressed in work and profession?

Clearly, Paul recognizes that some gifts are temporary and momentary, such as speaking in tongues, but his argument to the Corinthians is to recognize that in addition to such gifts there are also gifts that are long-lasting, enduring, some even permanent. Most gifts do not appear and then disappear, but are manifest in a person's life for the purpose of building community. Charisms are gifts the Spirit grants, so it is according to the Spirit's graciousness for the sake of the community whether gifts are momentary or enduring. The essential theological claim is pneumatological: charisms speak to what the Spirit is doing and how the Spirit is present in community. Charisms are not manifest according to our desire for a certain gift or its duration. This is why Paul can claim that "the gifts and calling of God are irrevocable" (Rom 11:29).

Some gifts can be given for a long time or a lifetime as is evidenced in many people, especially those, for example, who celebrate golden anniversaries in marriage or who, like Dorothy Day, work tirelessly at a particular effort for the course of their entire life. It is also the case that the Spirit introduces new charisms in a person's life. It is not uncommon for a person, after working in an area for several years, to discover a new calling—what initially might be an inclination but begins to urge them toward a new endeavor. For example, I have a neighbor who has been a family practitioner for many years and was drawn to hospice care and recently sought certification in palliative care. He has changed his practice to include serving hospice patients two days a week. I also know a colleague, after many years as a computer scientist, who decided to study spirituality, and another friend who was a social worker has become a horse trainer. In each instance, the person experienced a new interest and felt a "call" toward other forms of service through their work. In each case the shift was accompanied by an awareness of a gift calling them forth for a new form of service.

Likewise, persons who lose a spouse or experience the dissolution of a marriage may discover charisms for a second marriage or gifts to live the single life. Certainly parents who become grandparents discover gifts for their new role, gifts that take them beyond that of parenting, into a new relationship to children and youth. In each case, new gifts are granted; the Spirit acts anew. As the psalmist sings, "When you send forth your spirit, they are created; and you renew the face of the ground" (Ps 104:30). In other words, charisms are not automatically imprinted on the soul at baptism, predetermining every aspect of our lives. Charisms seem to be the type of gift that the Spirits gives throughout our lives as the Spirit sees fit.

Is there a difference between a charism and a talent or are they the same reality? When we experience something as a gift we generally mean that there is a part of ourselves that we experience as somehow given to us without merit or effort on our part. It just is: we cannot be praised or blamed for the gift, we can only accept it and praise (or blame) the giver. In this sense, charisms and talents are often experienced in much the same way. Many people experience a talent as something "natural, " a particular aptitude to do something that they did not seek to acquire, but were "born with." We can say, then, that charisms and talents are experienced to some extent as given whether through nature or grace.

From a Christian perspective there is no difference, then, in the origin of a charism or talent, perhaps only in the timing: both are seen as having a divine source. Talents that we are born with, some of which seem to be genetically based in our family tree, can be named as God-given gifts, since God works through the created order to bring about the divine will and purposes. Charisms, those gifts that are granted during our lifetime, are but another way in which the Spirit graces us for the well-being of the Body. In a very real sense talents and charisms are incarnational gifts, a graced presence that becomes enfleshed in our lives. As theologian

Thomas O'Meara notes, "Since the Spirit and the Lord Jesus are one with Father-Creator, there can be no conflict between my God-given biological and psychological identity and the personal gift of the Spirit. My charismatic identity is not utterly different from my personality. Charisms find in people potentialities they can draw forth, for the Spirit does not ask people to be what they cannot be, to exist as they do not in the mind and plan of God."[14]

When we notice a talent in a child or young person, we tend to encourage it because we know that learning the skills and capacities related to a talent can become an important formative experience. People who exert themselves in various ways to gain both knowledge and skill in a talent over time may develop a certain degree or level of competence. But is it the same for a charism? We generally accept the idea that talents need to be shaped and formed, but do charisms? Is there any effort and skill required for this divine gift?

Another way of asking the question is: Do charisms come to us wholly and perfectly made or not? There are, of course, in history, prodigies that seem to be born with an overwhelming natural gift for some ability— Mozart's musical abilities, for example. But most people do not experience their talents and gifts in some perfect form, but rather as intimations toward some ability or capacity that mingles with an interest or passion. We tend to be attracted toward those things that we are "good at." Charisms are received as potentialities that must be accepted and formed into capacities, skills, and competencies. A charism, like a talent, lays a foundation for a certain capacity that develops, over time, into a patterned action. In other words, charisms are given and received but also need to be activated, cultivated, and formed into a capacity, a skill, or a competence. O'Meara notes that charisms are a "dialogue, a conversation between the Spirit and an individual Christian."[15] And in that dialogue, we are free to reject a charism, to not allow it to grow and change us and our lives.

Because charisms are a potential that are not yet fully developed, they require personal awareness, discernment, and acceptance. In discerning a gift and "pursuing" it, a person may need to acquire skills and abilities that allow the charism to develop to a fuller capacity. Charisms become the Spirit-gift of what I will later describe as "practices." Charisms are

---

[14] Ibid., 205.
[15] Ibid.

the Spirit-filled and Spirit-led capacities that develop over time into practices, the type of engaged, intentional action that make us into practitioners. In this process of discernment and learning, charisms require communal recognition and support, especially in regard to formation and education in both knowledge and ability. Finally, charisms require a context in which the gift can be "practiced" as a service for the community. In a certain sense they impose an obligation and responsibility on the recipient. They demand a response. Because freedom too is a gift, some persons are free to accept and use charisms or not. In a certain sense the denial of charisms, the rejection of God's call and gift, is a form of sin and self-rejection, but such a theological claim only makes sense if a person is in the position of choosing freely. Clearly, many people have gifts that are not recognized or cannot flourish in their community precisely because of control or oppression by others due to economic, social, or political conditions. Social and structural sin is a barrier to the flourishing of the Spirit's gifts in any community, but especially among the poor where there may be limited choices related to work, family, or relationships. Charisms are gifts that are intended to be given to the community. And yet, even in the most difficult and constrained circumstances, according to Paul, the Spirit is still granting people gifts for the well-being and upbuilding of the community. Clearly, many oppressed Christians, women and men, are inspired by the Spirit's love and granted charisms in their context to strive to surpass oppression through faithful discipleship.

Charisms and Life Commitments

Though Paul did not speak about charisms in relationship to what we have often called one's "state of life" or postbaptismal life commitments in marriage, celibacy, or the single life, the Catholic tradition has long emphasized these forms of adult faith commitments as deriving from a divine gift. Paul's main argument about charisms is in the context of various roles in the community, such as teaching or healing. It should not be difficult to recognize that each of these ways of life constitutes a calling for covenant-in-relationship, a commitment grounded in our baptism that draws us closer to and more deeply into the mystery of our faith. Each "how" of adult life is a further calling into communion for mission. In this sense, I am expanding the idea of charisms to include all parts of human life, including the way we live in marriage, celibacy, and single life.

A part of discovering our vocation in adulthood is discerning God's call in how to live through committed relationships. Most Christians discern a life commitment through one of three choices: marriage and family life, religious and/or intentional communities, or the single life. Each path entails a commitment to live in relationship in a particular way and to deepen and enrich one's life as a disciple in and through these relationships. The call in each path requires a continuing call of discipleship, especially new ways of embracing neighbor love, forgiveness, and stewardship. In choosing a path, the discernment of gifts and charisms to live fully these commitments is also required. How do we understand charism in relationship to each of these callings?

The charisms of marriage include gifts of lifelong fidelity to another person, a spouse, "in good times and in bad, in sickness and in health" until death separates the couple. Richard Gaillardetz discusses marriage as one path of the "life of communion" that is fostered through mutuality, companionship, and intimacy, what I will call marital charisms.[16] Mutuality in marriage is not just equality, Gaillardetz says, but requires us to "recognize and acknowledge the giftedness of the other." The charism of mutuality allows each person to help their spouse cultivate their gifts in marriage as well as in work and service. Companions are people with "whom a person shares bread," as Gaillardetz describes. The charism of companionship is the gift to live together, providing one another food and shelter, walking alongside each other every day. Intimacy is the charism of emotional closeness, vulnerability, and commitment to shed our false self to find our true self and to give that self to the other. Marital intimacy requires not just feeling good about the other, but grappling with the mystery of each person as a marriage forms and changes the self. Intimacy includes the charisms of sexual love, fidelity, and expression, as well as openness to parenting children and living as a family.

Wendy Wright explains that the charisms for parenting are an expression of a distinctive form of love, a generative love that calls parents (but not only parents) to "nurture children and raise up the next generation." She points out that this charism may be given to those who are not par-

---

[16] Richard Gaillardetz, *A Daring Promise: A Spirituality of Christian Marriage* (New York: Crossroad Publishing Co., 2002), 41–60.

ents, such as teachers or ministers. But with the parenting charism, the *"distilled* experience of parental love is discovered and cultivated most explicitly among those who raise children." But it is not automatic or experienced fully in all parents; it exists as a "potential gift," a "spirit-filled experience into which one is invited to grow. The lived experience of being a parent can provide opportunities for the heart to stretch and contour to the shape of this mature, generative love."[17]

Regarding the call to live in an intentional religious community, a person must discern both the charism of celibacy as well as the charism of the order or community. For example, a call to become a Franciscan involves discerning the charisms of Saint Francis' care for the poor and the earth; to become Benedictine involves discerning charisms for living in the cloister and praying the Liturgy of the Hours. As Donald Cozzens writes, "Some few men and women appear to possess the charism of celibacy, a graced call from God to pledge themselves to celibate living for the good of others and for the building up in history of the reign of God. For these individuals, celibacy is their *truth*—the right way for them to live out their lives."[18]

Charisms for the single life include the gifts of solitude as well as the gifts of friendship. Susan Muto describes the difference between alone-ness, loneliness, and solitude in the single life. The charism of single life is the transformation of a-loneness, "the pain of being alone," into solitude, which becomes rooted in solidarity and communion with others.[19] Out of a true solitude and aloneness, the single person lives fully into relationships of mutual love and concern for others.

I have named only a few charisms for each of these ways of life, which are not meant to be exhaustive or exclusive. Much more can be said about the charisms for each life commitment, but the point here is to show that the Spirit grants gifts to individuals as they heed the call to a particular way of life, gifts that can be long-lasting and enduring, sometimes ceasing or changing, but gifts nonetheless that are granted for building up the Body through a particular form of lifelong adult commitments.

[17] Wendy Wright, " The Charism of Parenting" in *Retrieving Charisms for the Twenty-First Century*, ed. Doris Donnelly (Collegeville, MN: Liturgical Press, 1999), 87ff.

[18] Donald Cozzens, *Freeing Celibacy* (Collegeville, MN: Liturgical Press, 2006), 21.

[19] Susan Annette Muto, *Celebrating the Single Life: A Spirituality for Single Persons in Today's World* (New York: Crossroad, 1984), 40.

Vocation as Service for Mission

A second facet of vocation involves the discernment of what I am called to do. "God brings everyone into this life to do something, to accomplish some mission, to make a positive contribution to the Body of Christ."[20] In the United States, a common answer to this question is related to work and labor, or career and profession. This is certainly an important aspect of vocation as service, but it is too narrow to claim that work for employment is the only legitimate way to define vocation as service. A vocation to service for mission includes both work through employment but also work and service that is nonemployed, where no financial exchange takes place, most often in our context through volunteer opportunities. Again, the important element here is a calling from God to utilize gifts in service for the good of the community.

In considering work and labor as vocation, it is important to point out that not all work is experienced or embraced as vocation. Work, either physical or mental, is a necessity for most people if they are to "make a living" and obtain the economic means to sustain their lives. Many people must accept work in order to support themselves and a family but it does not always mean that they find the work meaningful or experience it as a calling. Work can be a necessity, with little free choice or flexibility, even experienced as drudgery and painful (Gen 3:17-19). Furthermore, those who find themselves fortunate enough to choose the work they do may see work as a calling, but that is not always the case. Some people find themselves in a job for which they are competent, but in which they are not living out the fullness of their gifts.

For work to be experienced as a Christian vocation, a person recognizes that they have certain gifts and capacities, talents they are born with as well as charisms freely granted by the Spirit, that they seek to express through work that becomes a form of service for the larger good. For work to be a calling means it is recognized as both a gift and a response. It is more than a desire to do something for others; it is felt as an imperative that I must do this, regardless of how difficult. In that sense work is experienced as a calling that brings both joy and fulfillment.

A common way to think about work in Western societies is by having a career or profession. The root meaning of the word "profession" is "to profess," "testify on behalf of," "stand for," or to "avow." The professions historically have been grounded in a covenant that both shapes and

---

[20] Marie Theresa Coombs and Francis Kelly Nemeck, *Called By God: A Theology of Vocation and Lifelong Commitment* (Collegeville, MN: Liturgical Press, 1992), 3.

constrains the practitioner, determining to a large extent what they can and cannot do in service for another. For example, lawyers make a promise to uphold the Constitution and to represent their clients fairly and justly, and physicians uphold the Hippocratic oath and promise to "do no harm."

We can often fail to see the way in which our work or professions are a means by which we serve God and others. Or at least it is not common to ask people to express how their work is a Christian vocation. In a small book of essays, *Professions of Faith: Living and Working as a Catholic,* a group of adult Catholics articulate how they experience their professions, as well as marriage and parenting, as a "profession of faith," a vocation. David Armitage, an architect, describes encountering God as architect: "My life as an architect began—as all things began—with the story of Genesis, with God's creation of the world. . . . Since childhood, I have found the image of God as architect of the universe immensely compelling. . . . Few images show God so *at work,* so *human,* as these images."[21] A Catholic police officer writes of how difficult it is to live out the fundamentals of faith especially regarding the dignity of all peoples, even criminals, and how his calling as a police officer is one of love, service, and obedience. Lives of service through teaching, medicine, social work, acting, writing, and practicing law all demonstrate how discipleship matters in the day-to-day lives of working people, even in a secular society that does not always honor "jobs" as vocation.

There are also many forms of service and work that do not come under the category of profession or job or are connected to financial remuneration. Volunteering is an important form of service in U.S. society in both secular and religious communities. Many people give of their time and talents generously to meet the needs of others and many do so in response to gifts that they recognize from the Spirit: gifts for physical labor (Habitat for Humanity), organization and distribution of food and clothing (Red Cross, Catholic Charities), befriending the disadvantaged (Big Brothers Big Sisters), and visiting the sick or lonely (Befrienders Ministries). Wherever there is human need the Spirit bestows gifts in the community, both within and beyond the church, in order that these needs be met.

It is easy to see how Paul's lists of charisms correspond to roles in the community along the lines of work, profession, and community volunteer

---

[21] James Martin and Jeremy Langford, *Professions of Faith: Living and Working as a Catholic* (Franklin, WI: Sheed and Ward, 2002), 27.

service. Because charisms are capacities for action, they emerge through what we do, and embracing a form of service through professional or charitable organizations is an obvious way for Christians to live out their calling as disciples and discern their particular gifts of service. Charisms are gifts of the Spirit that serve particular human needs. When we live and work in response to charisms it is not without hardship and struggle, but it can be felt as a deep resonance that what I do and what I can offer is a true expression of who I am. I will return to this idea in chapters 4 and 5.

Who I Am: Vocation as Charism in Context

The third element of vocation has to do with who I am, self-identity, my "being" as a unique person. During a lifetime the sense of self, who I am, is deeply intertwined with the other two elements of vocation, the vocational how and what. As Coombs and Nemeck write, "Vocationally speaking, who we are, how we are becoming, and what we are sent to do initiate with God and redound with God. . . . [T]he Lord chooses us to be unique persons, to become ourselves in a certain manner and to bear fruit."[22] But we also have a sense that the self is distinct from our life commitments and our service; we experience ourselves as a "being" that is somehow transcendent to these particularities.

To attempt to understand this mystery, the authors describe vocation as both an eternal and a temporal reality. The eternal aspect of vocation refers to our calling before time, "in the womb" as Jeremiah claims (Jer 1:5), and extends beyond death and time into the "ever-deepening communion" with the Trinity that is God's eschatological promise. "In several respects, our eternal vocation corresponds to *who* the Lord is calling us to be. Who we are destined to be are unique persons transformed in God by God. Who we have been foreknown, chosen and called to be are singular individuals deified and divinized by participation in the life of the Trinity. This self-identity and transformation begin with inception and develop slowly throughout our earthly sojourn."[23] To speak of charism in terms of an eternal vocation, is to claim that the Spirit gifts us with the capacity for self-transcendent experience, understanding,

[22] Coombs and Nemeck, *Discerning Vocations to Marriage, Celibacy and Singlehood*, 10.
[23] Ibid., 9.

and longing to live in full communion with the divine beyond the here and now.

As creatures that live in time and space, our temporal vocation focuses on who I am in relationship to the how and the what we do for God and others in our earthly life. In time and place, who we are must be discerned and understood within the context of our lives, not outside existence in an idealized realm. In one regard who I am is very particular and not universal: I was born in a family of Irish immigrants, farmers in Iowa, Catholic and Protestant; I am a woman, a "Caucasian" on the U.S. census form, and I have lived my whole life in North America in a "middle-class" household; I have back problems. In other words, I cannot understand myself or my identity outside the categories of family, place, gender, race, economics, and the body. Vocation in its temporal form is always a calling in context. We experience God's presence and calling within the very concrete, daily facets of our existence.

What I am describing in personal terms are common themes among theologians who explore issues of the human person and what it means to be made in the image of God. The self, as understood in contemporary theological anthropology, is a person-in-relation in time and history, place and culture, body and gender. As U.S. Hispanic theologian Miguel Diaz notes, "God reveals what humans can perceive. In this sense, we can metaphorically speak of the human and the divine as being caught up in an eternal nuptial dance in which God is always initiating. But God does not invite us to dance by singing to us in a 'language' we cannot comprehend. Rather, God sings to us tunes that are capable of moving us to the dance floor. The songs that God sings contain human lyrics, rhythms, and melodies. Simply put, the encounter with grace is always a human encounter."[24] Naming this divine song and dance in language we can understand means for Diaz and other contextual theologians that grace is encountered in and through social and cultural realities. Our identities are forged through the cultural constructs such as race and ethnicity, gender and the body, and economics and politics, which means that encountering God in the world is to encounter God through our experiences shaped by these realities. There is not some form of personhood to be discovered outside contextual realities since each person is born, lives, and discerns a sense of self within their actual lives. To speak

---

[24] Miguel Diaz, *On Being Human: U.S. Hispanic and Rahnerian Perspectives* (Maryknoll, NY: Orbis Books, 2001), 24.

of charisms of the self in this regard is to acknowledge the Spirit's gift to live fully who I am within my time and place, to be shaped by it as well as to strive to create a community within history that allows full human flourishing for others.

Nevertheless, part of the mystery of human existence includes the realization that I am not entirely determined by cultural, social, and embodied realities. In experiences of relationship and communion, freedom, self-determination, creativity, and the struggle against oppressive constructs of the self and others, persons experience their being in relationship to the divine source of grace that grounds existence and calls it forth into ever more human fullness. Every human encounter is an encounter with a graced reality in relationship to us. As Karl Rahner notes, we are created as "hearers" of the Word, and as Diaz extends Rahner's idea, we are hearers, seers, and doers of the Word.[25]

The image of the human person commonly claimed today is that we are fundamentally relational, made in relationship and for relationship. In philosophical terms, the Orthodox theologian John Zizioulas claims that "there is no true being without communion."[26] In other words, "to be" is identical with "to be in relation," the self is fundamentally relational. As Roberto Goizueta notes the "community is the birthplace of the self." Relationships constitute the self, they are "the most basic form of human action since through relationship, we discover and live out our identity as intrinsically relational beings."[27] And to claim that human relationality is essential to the self correlates with the insight that God is Trinity, persons in communion, a God constituted by relationship. This divine communion grounds our identity and relationships because we are made in the image of this triune God.

The charisms of the self for relationality are those gifts that comprise our capacity for response, to be fully in relationship to both neighbor and God. Relational charisms are manifest in encountering each person as a graced reality, not as object or nonperson, stranger or outsider, but as a self-in-relation in time and place, part of what Alejandro Garcia-Rivera calls "a horizontal fellowship of creaturely differences."[28] In other

---

[25] Ibid., 117.

[26] John D. Zizioulas, *Being as Communion: Studies in Personhood and the Church* (Crestwood, NY: St. Vladimir's Seminary Press, 1985), 18.

[27] Roberto Goizueta, *Caminemos Con Jesús: Toward a Hispanic/Latino Theology of Accompaniment* (Maryknoll, NY: Orbis Books, 1995), 33.

[28] Quoted in Diaz, *On Being Human*, 52.

words, relationality recognizes the diverse differences of persons who experience grace through culture, language, and embodied experience. A charism of the self-in-relation does not erase these particularities or consider them extrinsic to other selves, but rather welcomes them as part of the graced experience of the "other." Likewise, charisms of the self-in-relation are gifts that allow us to encounter, receive, and celebrate all living creatures, nature, the earth, and cosmos as related to us but distinct. Zizioulas expresses the interdependence and relational distinctiveness through the idea that each "person is otherness in communion and communion in otherness."

Discipleship is a personal, social, and vocational identity, rooted in Christ and context. Who I am as a disciple, along with how I live and what I do, are forged within a time and place, and it is in that context that the Spirit discerns the gifts needed for the flourishing of the community and grants the community those gifts. The Spirit of God breathes life into all creation at the beginning, and continues to renew, inspire, and empower all of life throughout history. The broad and expansive work of the Spirit becomes particular and concrete in each human life and context: charisms are a way of describing that particularity and contextuality of the grace-fullness of the Spirit in the here and now. Such a claim also implies that there is a demand on both persons and their communities to search out, discern, test, and form charisms into service for the common good. Charisms are manifest in who a person is and what they do: they hold identity and action together in a person's life. They are the God-given energy and direction for relationship, communion, and mission. Though they are particular in each person, the call to service through the Spirit's gifts unite Christians into one Body.

Sources for Further Reading

Allegretti, Joseph G. *Loving Your Job, Finding Your Passion: Work and the Spiritual Life*. Mahwah, NJ: Paulist Press, 2000.

Boff, Leonardo. *Church, Charism and Power: Liberation Theology and the Institutional Church*. New York: Crossroad, 1985.

Coombs, Marie Theresa, and Francis Kelly Nemeck. *Called By God: A Theology of Vocation and Lifelong Commitment.* Collegeville, MN: Liturgical Press, 1992.

———. *Discerning Vocations to Marriage, Celibacy and Singlehood.* Collegeville, MN: Liturgical Press, 1994.

Cozzens, Donald. *Freeing Celibacy.* Collegeville, MN: Liturgical Press, 2006.

Diaz, Miguel. *On Being Human: U.S. Hispanic and Rahnerian Perspectives.* Maryknoll, NY: Orbis Books, 2001.

Dillon, Richard J. "Speaking of Authority and Charism from the New Testament." In *Raising the Torch of Good News: Catholic Authority and Dialogue with the World,* edited by Bernard P. Prusak, 3–12. Lanham, MD: University Press of America, 1986.

Donnelly, Doris, ed. *Retrieving Charisms for the Twenty-First Century.* Collegeville, MN: Liturgical Press, 1999.

Downey, Michael. *Altogether Gift: A Trinitarian Spirituality.* Maryknoll, NY: Orbis Books, 2000.

Dulles, Avery. "Earthen Vessels: Institution and Charism in the Church." In *Above Every Name: The Lordship of Christ and Social Systems,* edited by Thomas E. Clark, 155–87. Ramsey, NJ: Paulist Press, 1980.

Fragomeni, Richard N. *Come to the Light: An Invitation to Baptism and Confirmation.* New York: Continuum, 1999.

Gaillardetz, Richard R. *A Daring Promise: A Spirituality of Christian Marriage.* New York: Crossroad, 2002.

Goizueta, Roberto. *Caminemos con Jesús: Toward a Hispanic/Latino Theology of Accompaniment.* Maryknoll, NY: Orbis Books, 1995.

Haughey, John C. *Converting Nine to Five: A Spirituality of Daily Work.* New York: Crossroad, 1989.

———. *Revisiting the Idea of Vocation: Theological Explorations.* Washington, DC: The Catholic University of America Press, 2004.

Martin, James, and Jeremy Langford, eds. *Professions of Faith: Living and Working as a Catholic.* Franklin, WI: Sheed and Ward, 2002.

Muto, Susan Annette. *Celebrating the Single Life: A Spirituality for Single Persons in Today's World.* New York: Crossroad, 1989.

Neafsey, John. *A Sacred Voice Is Calling: Personal Vocation and Social Conscience.* Maryknoll, NY: Orbis Books, 2006.

Placher, William C., ed. *Callings: Twenty Centuries of Christian Wisdom on Vocation.* Grand Rapids, MI: Wm. B. Eerdmans, 2005.

Searle, Mark. *Christening: The Making of Christians.* Collegeville, MN: Liturgical Press, 1980.

Seasoltz, R. Kevin. *God's Gift Giving: In Christ and Through the Spirit.* New York: Continuum, 2007.

Schmitt, Harley H. *Many Gifts, One Lord.* Minneapolis, MN: Augsburg Fortress Press, 1993.

Schwehn, Mark R., and Dorothy C. Bass, eds. *Leading Lives that Matter: What We Should Do and Who We Should Be.* Grand Rapids, MI: Wm. B. Eerdmans, 2006.

Schuurman, Douglas J. *Vocation: Discerning Our Callings in Life.* Grand Rapids, MI: Wm. B. Eerdmans, 2004.

Sullivan, Francis A. *Charisms and Charismatic Renewal: A Biblical and Theological Study.* Ann Arbor, MI: Servant Books, 1982.

Volf, Miroslav. *After Our Likeness: The Church as the Image of the Trinity.* Grand Rapids, MI: Wm. B. Eerdmans, 1998.

Zizioulas, John D. *Being as Communion: Studies in Personhood and the Church.* Crestwood, NY: St. Vladimir's Seminary Press, 1985.

Chapter 3

Vocation to Ministry:
Leadership in the Christian Community

Vocation is a life lived in response to the following questions: Who am I? How do I live? What service do I offer to the world? In this chapter I begin the discussion of ministry as vocation by focusing on the question of service. First, I want to clarify the relationship between disciples and ministers by what distinguishes them from each other and by their mutual interdependence.[1] Second, I offer a broad definition of ministry to help delineate the particular service rendered by ministers in the community. By examining what ministry is, we can better understand the charisms and practices that we discern in the vocation to ministry. By considering ministry through the charisms for service distinctive to this vocation, I hope to show that questions of who emerge in and through the practice of ministry. The question "who am I?" cannot be answered prior or separately from the question of "what service do I offer to the world?"

As I mentioned in the preface, the how question in terms of marriage, celibacy, or single life has a long and complicated history as each relates to ministry. In the Catholic community the call to ordained ministry for men determines the how of one's vocation: priests are required by canon law to live a life of celibacy. Protestant reformers rejected the law of celi-

---

[1] Many of the ideas on discipleship and ministry in this chapter were developed in conversation with James Nieman. See Kathleen A. Cahalan and James Nieman, "Mapping the Field of Practical Theology," in *For Life Abundant: Practical Theology, Theological Education, and Christian Ministry*, eds. Craig Dykstra and Dorothy C. Bass (Grand Rapids, MI: Eerdmans, 2008), 62–85.

bacy and decided that marriage and ministry were not incompatible. The Orthodox community does not mandate celibacy for its priests, but it does for its bishops. Each tradition has particular ways of thinking about how a person lives their postbaptismal commitments in relationship to the practice of ministry. I am bracketing this set of questions and issues and invite the reader, from within their tradition, to consider how the practice of ministry, as defined here, helps to illuminate the question of how a minister will live their postbaptismal commitments.

Disciples and Ministers

As I have argued thus far, discipleship is the self-identity and shared calling common to all members of the Christian community. Disciples are constituted in baptism as followers of Christ, an immersion that personally, vocationally, and socially "orders" their relationships to God and neighbor in a new way. As John Zizioulas claims, "there is no such thing as 'non-ordained' persons in the Church" because baptism places us within a new set of relationships at the outset.[2] Our lives are reordered in Christ to one another.

Vocation is a distinctive calling arising from discipleship through the Spirit's gifts of charisms. Vocation is manifest in each Christian life, at least to the extent that a person responds to and develops their charisms in response to God's initiative. Vocation, then, is neither reserved for a few nor limited to one set of possibilities. It is imperative to the self-identity of each disciple to understand their life, their whole of life, in terms of vocation.

What this understanding of vocation means for a minister is that ministry is a distinct vocation among many vocations that exist within the Christian community. And, as with any vocation, ministry does not replace or supplant the self-identity or lived reality of discipleship. Rather, it is a further realization of the call to discipleship in and through a distinctive set of charisms. The self-identity of the minister is rooted in discipleship and the further deepening of that identity takes place by living the demands of discipleship in and through the vocation to ministry.

There is no vocation that exceeds other vocations, and that is certainly the case for ministry, which oftentimes in the Christian tradition has been

---

[2] Zizioulas, *Being as Communion*, 215.

defined as the highest or the only vocation. But ministry is not a higher or holier calling. It is a distinctive calling, but then again all vocations are distinctive from each other and each requires a full-blown explanation of the gifts and charisms that shape a person's self-identity and service in particular ways.

What, then, is the vocation to ministry? Stated simply, and to be expanded upon in the next section, *ministry is the vocation of leading disciples in the life of discipleship for the sake of God's mission in the world.* This means, in terms of the definition of vocation, that the self-identity of the minister is grounded firmly in discipleship and in the call to lead disciples; what ministers do in terms of leading discipleship is their primary service in the community, and how they live in terms of their postbaptismal commitments must be integrated with who they are and what they do as minister. If there is anything unique about the vocation of ministry it is that it is directly related to the flourishing of discipleship in the Christian community and in the world. And in this regard ministers are in a unique position to care about and for the vocation of all Christians.

Thus far I have been making the claim that ministers are disciples. The minister takes on a different set of relations in the community by virtue of being a minister, but they never cease to embody and embrace the features of discipleship. Richard Gaillardetz identifies the movement into ministry as "ecclesial repositioning." He acknowledges that baptism is the fundamental call to a life of service, but that ordination, or other ritual acts that signify the minister's new relationship to the community such as installation or commissioning, never replace baptism but are rooted in baptism. Ministers remain disciples but by virtue of their calling to the vocation of leading disciples they assume a new relationship to the community. In becoming a minister, they do not relinquish discipleship, nor do they become some other kind of Christian by virtue of their call to ministry. They do not live according to another set of features. They share in the same fundamental call and vocation as all Christians: the call to follow Christ.

This is why the claim that ministers are disciples is such an important point: they are not some final, fully realized, or finished disciple. They have not achieved some higher level of discipleship. Ministers seek to be faithful, trustworthy disciples in the same way that all disciples do. Of course, because of their calling into leadership in the Christian community, a minister's discipleship is more visible and at times transparent; it becomes a public sign and witness by virtue of their leadership role. Ministers become a sign of authentic discipleship and disciples naturally look to them for cues and clues into this deep mystery. Disciples are right to look to ministers for how to live the life of discipleship, but they can also place unrealistic burdens on ministers if they expect them to live as perfect disciples. Their lives are *a* sign, one among many, to be sure, in the community, of what discipleship means. And yet all disciples are to be a sign and witness of discipleship. Ministers cannot bear the burden of being *the* sign for the community. Such expectation only leads to ego-ism, pride, or burnout on the part of ministers, and disciples who place their ministers on pedestals of holiness are probably ignoring the de-mands of their own call.

There is an important second and related point: while ministers are disciples, disciples are not ministers. I make this claim with great sensi-tivity because I want to argue that disciples do not, generally, carry out ministry as vocation. In the terms I've spelled out thus far: discipleship is a shared calling and vocation is the particular calling that arises from charisms. Ministry is one particular vocation among many because the Spirit gives to some the charisms for ministry. Likewise, the vocation to parenting is not given to all, nor are the charisms to be a lawyer or judge, a nurse or social worker, a farmer or plumber. To say that disciples are not ministers is not to imply that disciples do not have a vocation or are not called into service. It is to claim that the community of disciples is made up of many different vocations and ministry is but one of those vocations.

I am offering a counterperspective to what has become a common way of speaking about the baptismal call to service in many Christian com-munities. I recognize that many churches use the language of ministry to emphasize that every Christian life is rooted in service and that all Christians share in the church's mission. All Christian vocation, then, is defined as ministry. I think there are at least two reasons for this height-ened use of "ministry" in recent times to refer to the service of all Chris-tians, one related to biblical scholarship on the term *diakonia* and the second related to churches seeking to overcome the division and hier-archy between clergy and laity.

Biblical scholars came to recognize that the term *diakonia*, commonly translated as "ministry," refers largely to the service of all Christians but had long been interpreted as applying only to ministers. It is commonly accepted that the type of service Jesus calls his followers to embrace is meant for all, not just the apostles or the Twelve.[3] For example, Jesus

---

[3] Studies of ministry in the New Testament conclude that the use of the term "Twelve" is a symbol of the twelve tribes of Israel. The term "apostles" is sometimes used in reference to the Twelve, but after the time of Jesus it pertained to more than

says, "For the Son of Man came not to be served but to serve, and to give his life a ransom for many" (Mark 10:45), and the author of 1 Peter writes, "Like good stewards of the manifold grace of God, serve one another with whatever gift each of you has received" (1 Pet 4:10). To translate certain New Testament references to *diakonia* as applying to ministers or church leaders is a distortion of the text and its meaning, as is possible in these two examples. Biblical exegesis of *diakonia* freed the idea of Christian service from referring to the activity of ministers and pointed to Jesus' call that all Christians live a life of service.

A second reason for reclaiming service as ministry for all Christians has been motivated in recent times by churches seeking to overcome the centuries-long divide between clergy and laity, in which the laity are stationed as passive recipients of the clergy's ministry. In the twentieth century, both Protestants and Catholics have worked to change distortions in their theologies of the laity, in particular emphasizing the laity's vocation to transform the world and to be engaged as "full, active and conscious participants" in the life of the church.[4]

Two examples, both from the 1980s, express the idea that all Christians are called to ministry, in the broadest sense of Christian service, and some are called to ministry in a particular sense, notably ordained ministry. The World Council of Churches, in its groundbreaking 1982 document, *Baptism, Eucharist and Ministry*, defines ministry in the broadest sense as "the service to which the whole people of God is called, whether as individuals, as a total community, or as the universal Church." In addition, ministry or ministries "can also denote the particular institutional forms which this service may take" such as ordained ministry that "refers to persons who have received a charism and whom the church appoints for service by ordination through the invocation of the Spirit and the laying on of hands."[5] This important ecumenical statement expresses a theology of service and ministry that remains widely shared across Christian churches today.

---

twelve individuals and generally referred to those who were a witness to the risen Christ and had received a commission to go forth and proclaim the gospel. On the distinction between the Twelve and apostles, see John F. O'Grady, *Disciples and Leaders*, 67–74.

[4] *Sacrosanctum Concilium*, 14. See *Vatican Council II: Volume I, The Conciliar and Post-Conciliar Documents*, ed. Austin Flannery (Northport, NY: Costello Publishing Company, 1975).

[5] World Council of Churches, *Baptism, Eucharist and Ministry*, Faith and Order Paper No. 111 (1982).

Richard McBrien is one of the first Catholics to offer a formal definition of ministry. In 1987, he wrote: "Ministry is rooted in the Holy Spirit; there is a distinction between general and particular ministry; all ministry is functional, that is, for the benefit of others, not primarily for the benefit of the minister; and ultimately all ministry is for the sake of the Kingdom of God, which is the object of the Church's mission."[6] For McBrien, Christian ministry has two levels: the universal level that is the service "to others in Christ and because of Christ" and the specific level in which service is offered in the name of the Church and for the sake of its mission. Specific ministry is designated by the church.

Both of these definitions emphasize two forms or expressions of Christian ministry, the first as service that is carried forth by the whole church, and the second as a form of specialized service carried out by some members that are designated primarily through ordination. At its best, the broadening of the term "ministry" is meant to be an inclusive, non-hierarchical, and nonauthoritarian way of defining ecclesial relationships. Yet, some see confusion when the term ministry is applied to everyone. What makes the vocation to ministry a distinct vocation in the community if everyone does ministry? How do communities distinguish between the ministry of disciples and the ministry of church leaders, particularly when most ecclesial leaders are ordained, educated, employed, and held to professional standards? Is there any reason for holding to a distinction between the service rendered through discipleship and the service we expect of the minister?

I acknowledge that my argument to reserve the language of "minister" and "ministry" for a particular vocation of leadership in the ecclesial community may be viewed as a historical throwback or unnecessary debate about terms. I think, however, it is important for several reasons. First, there is evidence among biblical scholars that the term *diakonia*, over the course of the first century, began to refer to the particular ministry of designated leaders.[7] In the book of Acts, Luke points to the role of the apostles and the Twelve in proclaiming the good news, and following in Jesus' ministry of preaching, healing, and teaching converts to be disciples (Acts 1:1-14; 6:1-7). He describes Paul's call to "ministry" in the power of the Spirit (Acts 20:24), as does Paul himself in his writings (1 Cor 3:5).

---

[6] Richard P. McBrien, *Ministry: A Theological, Pastoral Handbook* (San Francisco, CA: Harper and Row, 1987), 11.

[7] John N. Collins, *Are All Christians Ministers?* (Collegeville, MN: Liturgical Press, 1992), 35–45.

In addition to the category of disciples, gospel writers refer to apostles and the Twelve, and the roots of ministry as a designated service in the community has its roots in Jesus' call to these particular disciples. In Greek usage, "apostle" is a common term that means messenger, and the gospel writers use the term primarily to refer to those disciples that Jesus calls forth and sends out as messengers to proclaim the gospel, expel demons, and heal the sick (Mark 3:13-15; Matt 10:1-4; Luke 6:12-16). In some instances, however, the terms "disciples" and "apostles" are used interchangeably in the gospels, and there are several instances where disciples are called forth and sent in mission, such as Luke's story of the Seventy (Luke 10:1-10). Like "service," the category of disciple and apostle is more fluid in its earliest expressions, and only begins to take on more particular meanings as the community grows and changes.

The term "apostle," after the resurrection, is reserved for those who have experienced the risen Christ, which is why Paul can lay claim to the title (1 Cor 4:9-12; 15:7; 2 Cor 11:23-28). The distinctive calling of the apostles initially is as messengers and coworkers with Jesus in his ministry and then, in the absence of Jesus, as witnesses to the truth of the resurrection. The mission they receive is to continue Jesus' ministry by extending the call to follow as Jesus. The pattern is the same: the ministry that apostles are to take up is one of calling disciples to follow Christ (not themselves), gathering the people together in community for worship and teaching, and sending them forth into service. The apostles, and the other ministers called to serve in local communities, saw it as their vocation to continue Jesus' mission, through the power of the Holy Spirit, as the mission of the church. By the end of the first century, patterns of leadership and names are given to people in particular roles, such as elder, prophet, *episkopio*, presbyter, and deacon, drawn from specific Jewish and Roman contexts. The community began to ordain these leaders through the ritual of the laying on of hands, recognizing in them the charisms for leadership of disciples. Ministry, then, emerges in the postresurrection community as a service of leadership on behalf of the community. But the roots of this designated service lie in the call for all Christians to a life of service. It was not meant to be a form of service that replaces the disciples' call to service: ministry as service exists in order that disciples live a life of service.

I have argued that discipleship is a call and service that is expressed through the seven features of discipleship and that vocation is a particular calling and service in adulthood that arises from the Spirit's charisms. It is not a diminishment of discipleship to name what disciples do as discipleship. I have wondered whether the attempt to define all Christian service as ministry is a way to lift up the laity onto a higher plane, supporting the long-standing bias that ministry is a higher and holier calling that brings one closer to God. But, in fact, the baptized do not need to have ministry added to the features of discipleship to emphasize a higher ecclesial status. The highest calling, if "highest" is a legitimate category at all, is that of discipleship.

Disciples do offer service for the community through the life of discipleship and through their vocational callings. Ministers are disciples who receive particular charisms for practicing ministry and we should reserve the term for persons we deem the Spirit has blessed with these particular gifts. Before turning to consider the charisms for the practices of ministry in the next chapter, I want to offer a detailed definition of ministry.

Defining Ministry

> *Ministry is leading disciples through the practices of teaching, preaching, worship, pastoral care, social ministry, and administration; for the sake of discipleship lived in relationship to God's mission; as a public act discernable in word, deed, and symbol; on behalf of a Christian community; as a gift received through faith and baptism, charism, and vocation that is acknowledged by the community in rituals of commissioning, installation, and ordination; and as a practice that exists within a diverse array of ecclesial contexts, roles, and relationships.*

Obviously, the definition is long and cumbersome and cannot be easily repeated or captured in a slogan. As noted before, ministry is not a term that has been defined often and probably for good reason. But my definition is long and extensive because ministry is an enormous and complex reality, a practice that has existed for two thousand years in the Christian tradition, and is expressed in many ways in a wide variety of churches and contexts. In Catholic theology and practice "ministry" is a fairly recent term. Most Catholics considered ministry, at least prior to the Second Vatican Council, to refer to Protestant church leaders. Protestant communities operated with the assumption that ministry was what pastors did, which was probably quite obvious to everyone in the community. Today ministry is used widely to refer to both ordained and nonordained persons serving in churches, and I am using it in this general sense; each ecclesial tradition determines the roles, offices, and titles given to its ministers.

Definitions appear, at least among theologians, when long-held assumptions begin to be called into question or when a term is disputed. The definitions cited above have emerged at a point in history when Christian communities have been struggling with what is happening to ministry and the church in postmodern cultures. There have been dramatic changes in the past thirty years, most notably in the decline of vocations to ordained ministry among both Protestants and Catholics. At the same time, there has been a considerable increase in laypersons experiencing a call to ministry and now serving in large numbers, especially in the Catholic community, but also among Protestants. It is also the case that many young people today grow up with little awareness of what ministry is, what ministers do, and what constitutes a vocation to ministry, which often includes those who attend a church. When a reality is contested, diminished, or unknown, definitions help to sort out what is and is not essential.

However, I offer this definition with some caution. It is not meant to define once and for all or exactly what ministry is, but rather to describe and identify its primary characteristics. It is an invitation to think about what ministry is and in doing so to invite further considerations, amendments, and clarifications. It offers a rationale for why we continue to promote and educate for ministry, and why it is an essential vocation within the Christian community. For those discerning the call to ministry, the definition is meant to help in sorting out their vocation: is leadership for the sake of discipleship what I am called to do?

It is important to note that my definition rests on the definitions offered previously, but especially the work of Thomas O'Meara in his book *Theology of Ministry*. He identifies the primary characteristics of ministry, drawn from the New Testament and apostolic churches, as "doing something, for the advent and presence of the Kingdom of God, in public, on behalf of a Christian community, as a gift received in faith, baptism, ordination, and as an activity with its own limits and identity existing within a diversity of ministerial actions."[8] My definition roughly corresponds to O'Meara's basic claims but expands and elaborates them in an effort to further clarify ministry. I will consider the definition in each of its parts.

---

[8] O'Meara, *A Theology of Ministry*, 141.

Ministry Is Leading Disciples

Though the New Testament does not use the term "leaders" or "leadership," we think of those who took up the challenge of continuing Jesus' ministry, the apostles who founded and organized communities in the Roman Empire, who preached and taught the faith, as leaders. In contemporary terms, leaders are defined as those people who are in a position of responsibility for a group, effort, or organization in guiding it to serve its primary purposes. Definitions of leadership today describe leaders as people who persuade and influence others to carry out a common purpose, who are given the authority to direct people and resources, who are called upon to give vision and meaning to a collective effort.

The primary purpose of ministry is that ministers are called upon to persuade and influence disciples to live out the features of discipleship and in so doing participate in God's mission. As leaders, ministers have authority to "oversee" the community so that its gifts and resources are used for the mission into which they have been baptized. Ministers help disciples see a vision for the Christian life, the already and not yet character of existence, and interpret that vision, through the Scriptures and tradition, by offering compelling and meaningful ways to understand and live the faith in context.

Leadership in Christian ministry is not a service rendered for self-advancement or to exercise power and authority over others but a service of offering one's gifts for the sake of building up the community. The Spirit blesses some persons with the gifts of ministry in order that discipleship might thrive and flourish. Ministers are called to lead disciples because discipleship is the way in which followers of Christ come into full fellowship with God and their neighbor and pursue God's mission in the world. Ministry exists not to further itself but to further discipleship for the sake of mission.

Through the Practice of Teaching, Preaching, Worship, Pastoral Care, Social Ministry, and Administration

In Christian ministry, leadership is carried forth through a set of practices that are particular to ministry. Leadership is not a separate charism or practice but rather is enacted and embodied in and through these six practices. I will discuss the Christological and pneumatological basis for each practice in the next chapter. How can we first understand these six practices in relationship to discipleship?

Ministry arises from discipleship for the sake of discipleship. One of the reasons that discipleship and ministry look so similar is that the charisms for ministry are directly related to the seven features of discipleship. That is, what ministers do in ministry looks a lot like what Christians do in living discipleship. I am claiming, then, that there is direct correspondence between the features of discipleship and the practices of ministry. The central practices of ministry arise directly from discipleship and exist to further the life of discipleship:

1. To become a follower means to learn to follow in the way of Christ, to embrace Jesus as follower of Abba's way and teacher of Abba's kingdom. Ministers are teachers who help disciples learn the path of discipleship, its joys and its risks. Teaching, evangelization, and catechesis arise from being a follower.

2. To become a worshiper means to join together with Christ in praise of Abba, to join with a worshiping community to lift up voices of praise and thanksgiving. Ministers preside over the community's prayer and worship in order that the community's worship might unify the community as one body. Leading worship and prayer arise from the call to be a worshiper.

3. To practice being a witness means to tell others what God has done for us in Christ. Ministers are the church's witness through the ministry of preaching. The ministry of preaching arises from disciples' call to give witness and testimony.

4. To embrace the practice of forgiveness and neighbor love means to learn the dynamics of sin and grace, evil and redemption, death and new life. Ministers accompany disciples as a spiritual guide, offering care, healing, and guidance, particularly in times of pain and suffering. Pastoral care arises from the call to practice neighbor love and forgiveness of self and others.

5. Likewise to be a neighbor to the stranger and the outcast, to be a prophet regarding the poor and the alien, requires leaders who can help the community discern, organize, and call forth prophetic responses to the cries of the poor. Social ministry and outreach arises from the call to be a prophetic neighbor.

6. To tend the goods of the earth and all creation, the community requires administration, management, and oversight of its material and spiritual goods. Ministers lead by administering and governing the community's resources, which arises from the demands of stewardship.

The practices of ministry are distinctive from discipleship as forms of leadership but are deeply connected to discipleship, arising from discipleship for the sake of discipleship.

The New Testament provides a foundation for understanding ministry as Christological (rooted in Christ), pneumatological (gift of the Spirit), and ecclesial (called forth and designated by the community). Ministry is Christological because it flows from Jesus' ministry: Jesus is teacher, preacher, leader of prayer, healer and reconciler, prophet, and organizer of community. Jesus leads in and through these practices. He calls some disciples to be apostles in order to continue his ministry of teaching, preaching, and healing for the sake of the community. Ministry is Christological insofar as the minister is called to be a servant as Christ is servant, a servant who leads people to embrace God's radical call to discipleship. Ministry is Christological not because ministers become Christ in the community but because they are called to point the way to Christ so that all may live as *imago Christi*.

The way in which Jesus goes about "making disciples" is by teaching, preaching, leading in prayer, extending care and healing, calling for justice and mercy, and overseeing the goods of the community. By experiencing what he does, people come to know who he is; in other words, Jesus does not need to establish who he is by role, title, or office in order to demonstrate his authority and divine power. Rather, he boldly goes forth as preacher and healer in order that in and through his actions his followers (and enemies) come to realize who he is. It is only after experiencing his teaching and caring, his prophecy and prayer, that people name him Lord and Messiah.

It is similar with ministry and ministers. It is imperative to identify the charisms for ministry among these six practices when the community calls forth its leaders. When these gifts are discerned and formed through education and practice, a disciple has become a minister and assumes the role, title, or office appropriate to their gifts for service.

Ministry is also pneumatological. According to Paul, the church is constituted through charisms, gifts of the Spirit. This means that the Spirit constitutes the church through gifts of discipleship and vocation, including ministry. The gifts for teaching the faith, preaching the gospel, presiding at worship, offering pastoral care, developing social ministries and outreach to the needy, and organizing and governing the community are all based in gifts of the Spirit for each particular practice. When we discern gifts for ministry, we are looking for those people and gifts related to these practices.

Ministry is also ecclesial not because ministers are "head" of the church, but because their gifts of leadership for the sake of discipleship are recognized, called forth, and "ordained" by the community. Ministry is ecclesial because the community discerns the Spirit's gifts for ministry, calls forth these people, and commits to prepare them for service. The community has a responsibility to nurture and support ministry because it exists for its own good.

For the Sake of Discipleship Lived in Relationship to God's Mission

Many definitions of ministry point to the kingdom of God as the source and purpose of ministry. As O'Meara explains, "ministry has the clear purpose of serving the kingdom of God as brought and preached by Jesus. Ministry makes the kingdom explicit, turning its ambiguous presence into sacrament, word and action."[9] In contemporary theology, the kingdom or reign of God is interpreted to be God's will and mission for humanity and creation, the presence of God's mercy and justice, love and peace, manifested fully and completely in the eschaton and glimpsed incompletely in the present.

Clarifying the relationship between the reign of God and ministry is very important, since far too often Christians confuse ministry with bringing about the reign of God. This sentiment is most clearly seen in language that describes Christians as "building" or "bringing about" the kingdom through efforts to create a world of peace and justice. On the one hand, nothing could be farther from the truth. As Jesus teaches, the reign of God is sheer gift, both in its present and final reality, and no one, not even he knows the hour or the day (Mark 13:32). What we see and experience each day are glimpses of God's reigning presence, but its complete fullness is something we can only imagine and not fully know in the present. It is certainly not something we can bring about by working harder and we cannot manipulate God into bringing it about; we can ask for its coming—"your kingdom come"—and for readiness, but God's graced presence is a reality and gift that God grants freely and lovingly. Nothing we can do makes God bring about the kingdom, either in the present or the future.

On the other hand, if we are not about bringing God's kingdom to earth by our service, why heed the call to discipleship or ministry? If

---

[9] Ibid., 142.

God's kingdom is not a political party or social program, then "working" on behalf of the kingdom means following the way of God's reign, living in relationship to the fullness of God's redemptive presence, and responding to that graced reality in all that we encounter. The reign of God, as McBrien states, is the "will of God in force," it is God "past, present and future all at once" that is breaking into history and a future reality in its totality.[10] The life of discipleship is the call to live as God wills us into becoming one with the divine reality, and our efforts at neighbor love, reconciliation, prophetic words, deeds of justice, and stewardship of the earth is a response to the call of God to love what God loves and to live lives that reflect God's reigning presence in them. Ministry then is not motivated by a desire to get disciples busy building God's kingdom, it is motivated to help disciples recognize, receive, and respond to God's reigning presence in their lives and in the life of the world.

As a Public Act Discernable in Word, Deed, and Symbol

Because ministry is a practice it is constituted by intentional speech and action with a purpose. As we will see in following chapters, practices are intentional actions that have a purpose and aim. As I have shown, the purpose and aim of ministry is to foster disciples who participate in God's mission in the world. Because ministry is constituted by six basic practices, it should be fairly clear what ministers are doing when they do it. It is an enacted and embodied practice, and therefore shapes and forms a person continually into the identity of a minister. We will turn to this topic more fully in chapters 5 and 6.

On Behalf of a Christian Community

Ministry is not for its own sake. A minister does not have a call for their personal gain or self-gratification. As with any vocation, the charisms for ministry are given for the common good. Because the practices of ministry arise from and are practiced for the sake of discipleship, they embody who and what the community is for each other. In other words, as practices they bear a larger meaning than as a single act of an individual.

---

[10] McBrien, *Ministry*, 19.

In ministry, ministers serve as representatives of the community, *in persona ecclesia*.[11] And, as a representative they are a sign and symbol of the unity of the body. Through each of the practices, the minister acts on behalf of the community, as a sign and symbol of the community's commitment to its mission. For example, preachers give witness on behalf of the entire community, preaching is not their personal witness; administrators are granted the responsibility of overseeing all the goods of the community, but it is not their personal property; catechists are required to teach disciples what discipleship entails, which does not consist of their personal opinions or perspectives.

In becoming a representative of the community, however, the minister does not take over the seven practices of discipleship from disciples. Ministers do not replace disciples. One of the dangers of ministry that is evident in the tradition is distorted understandings of service. We find a plethora of images that place the minister in a superior relationship to the disciple; the disciple is defined as weak, incapable, ignorant, and without the possibility of salvation unless a minister is there to guide, teach, or save them from their sins. The pastor helps the helpless, the priest serves the laity, the teacher bestows knowledge on the ignorant, the physician of souls cures the sinner, and so on.

Of course, these ancient images capture something that is at the same time true. In fact, ministers do guide, teach, heal, and serve people, and many people are lost, ignorant, sinful, and helpless. The distortion arises from the subtle way in which these images place the minister and disciple as opposites, the God-bearer and the God-less juxtaposed one to another. In this picture the minister is standing *between* God and the disciple, presiding *over* disciples, and *replacing* rather than representing the community. They are not alongside the disciple or in the midst of the community of disciples.

What happens is that ministers can absorb all aspects of discipleship service into their roles and service. If not careful, they can assume discipleship from disciples rather than being a catalyst for discipleship. The danger in pitting the minister and the disciple as opposites translates service into a source of divine power that eventually moves toward paternalism and domination.

Both disciples and ministers must work together to maintain a proper perspective on what representation means and how it is enacted. To

---

[11] Susan K. Wood, *Sacramental Orders* (Collegeville, MN: Liturgical Press, 2000), 128–34.

represent the community means to lead through the practices of ministry to enhance, guide, and sustain the features of discipleship in order that disciples might live this reality more fully, not have it taken over or taken care of by the minister. Preaching exists within the community as a form of giving witness; it does not replace the demand on every Christian to give witness to their faith. Presiding at prayer and worship is a primary responsibility of the ordained minister but does not replace the demand that prayer and worship are first and foremost within the believer's life. So it is with pastoral care, administration, and catechesis. Chaplains assume responsibility for ministries of care, ensuring that every Christian who is sick, lonely, depressed, or dying is accompanied by the community. But the hospital chaplain or parish pastoral care coordinator represents but does not replace the community's responsibility to respond to their neighbor in times of suffering.

As a Gift Received through Faith and Baptism, Charism, and Vocation that is Acknowledged by the Community in Rituals of Commissioning, Installation, and Ordination

In the 1980s Edward Schillebeeckx, in his major scholarly examination of ministry, wrote that "Ministry in the church is not a status or state but a service, a function within the 'community of God' and therefore a 'gift of the Holy Spirit.'"[12] And in a revised version of the book a few years later, he states that ministry is "the specific crystallization of a universal charisma of the Spirit into a gift of the Spirit reserved for certain Christians with a function in the church."[13] Schillebeeckx's understanding of ministry is pneumatological: ministry is constituted by charisms for a particular function, or in the language that I prefer, a practice.

As a vocation, ministry is grounded in the gifts of faith and baptism, but emerge through charisms in adult life. Many young adults discern a call to ministry in two ways. First, some may have significant service experiences, perhaps in worship or a social justice setting, in which they become enthusiastic about their discipleship and they begin to claim that discipleship as their calling. Oftentimes this can lead to questions about whether they are called to lead disciples. A second way young people discern a call is when people in the community recognize that

[12] Edward Schillebeeckx, *Ministry: Leadership in the Community of Jesus Christ* (New York: Crossroad, 1981), 37.

[13] Edward Schillebeeckx, *The Church with a Human Face* (New York: Crossroad, 1985), 81.

they have particular gifts and invite them to explore and offer those gifts in the community, gifts for musical leadership, mentoring, justice advocacy, or serving as a catechist. Gifts are recognized by the community sometimes before a person recognizes them, and it is important that communities invite these gifts to be tried and tested, especially among young people. The discernment of true gifts must take place by both the person and the community.

The discernment to the vocation of ministry takes place over time and through various experiences. Gaillardetz describes five moments of a person's entry into ministry: (1) a personal call; (2) ecclesial discernment and recognition of a genuine charism; (3) formation appropriate to the demands of the ministry; (4) authorization by community leadership; (5) some ritualization (most often ordination) as a prayer for the assistance of the Holy Spirit and sending forth on behalf of community.[14]

As a person moves through the various paths of call, discernment, formation, authorization, and ritual blessing, they are "repositioned" in relation to members of the community. This ecclesial repositioning is not about standing above or over disciples, but standing in the midst of the body as one dedicated to "assemble and build up" the community.[15] Again, this language must be used carefully since discipleship exists as a reality *prior to* ministry, so the assembling and building up character of ministry does not mean starting from scratch. It means that a minister assumes responsibility for the gifts of faith, baptism, and discipleship in the community.

And as a Practice that Exists within a Diverse Array of Ecclesial Contexts, Roles, and Relationships

Not only is ministry a diverse practice, but it is practiced in diverse places, through different roles or offices, and with varying levels of education, responsibility, and ecclesial recognition. Diversity in ministry today is generally recognized and celebrated, though it marks a shift

---

[14] Richard Gaillardetz, "The Ecclesiological Foundations of Ministry within an Ordered Communion," in *Ordering the Baptismal Priesthood*, Susan K. Wood, ed. (Collegeville, MN: Liturgical Press, 2003), 36.

[15] "The chief responsibility of the ordained ministry is to assemble and build up the body of Christ by proclaiming and teaching the Word of God, by celebrating the sacraments, and by guiding the life of the community in its worship, its mission and its caring ministry" (*BEM*, II.13).

historically from the way ministry was practiced in the Catholic community when there were numerous priests and sisters in a parish carrying out sacramental and catechetical tasks, or in Protestant communities where full-time ordained ministers served in the majority of congregations. Today that landscape has changed: Catholics have welcomed permanent deacons since the early 1970s as well as lay ecclesial ministers. Both sets of ministers serve in a variety of roles, oftentimes taking leadership of one part of parish ministry, such as faith formation, sacramental preparation, liturgy, or social outreach. Some of these ministers work part-time, some full-time, some are paid and some not, some have education and some do not. Protestant ministers also serve in a variety of ministerial roles.

This is diversity in ministry today. What makes ministry a vocation is not the idea that all who are called to it are ordained to the priesthood or the pastorate, or that it is full-time and lifelong; what makes ministry a vocation is the charisms that constitute the practice, and what is accepted widely today is that this practice can take place across a spectrum of conditions and contexts.

Understanding diversity in ministry allows for disciples to serve as ministers in the congregation or community, as many do when they take up liturgical, catechetical, or pastoral care roles. In other words, this theology of ministry recognizes and allows for disciples to serve as ministers in particular circumstances. How is this possible if I am arguing for a distinction between discipleship and ministry? The charisms for ministry, as noted in chapter 2, are granted by the Spirit for the building up of the community. These gifts may be lifelong but they may also be given for a certain period of time, they may change or cease, or appear in mid- or late life. In other words, the charisms for ministry are granted by the Spirit, and it is up to the community to practice diligence in discerning their presence.

Take the example mentioned above, the young person becoming active in liturgical music or serving the homeless at a neighborhood soup kitchen. In my understanding, this is service through discipleship. The initial discernment of whether this is a call to ministry is not whether the person feels an inclination to do this service full-time or to be ordained, but rather whether they sense a call to lead disciples in pursuing this service. I think the questions of full-time ministry and ordination flow from this initial discernment. A teenager or young adult may discern that they enjoy playing music for a parish celebration, but that they do not see themselves serving as a music minister (paid or not). It may seem like a small distinction, but it is an important one. When disciples discern that they have a charism for one of the practices of ministry, serving as a eucharistic minister or lector or catechist, for example, they participate in ministry and embrace an identity as minister within this calling and context. They have discerned a charism for this practice.

Theologians have worked to describe and theologically explain diversity in ministry today. Edward Hahnenberg has developed a "concentric circle" model of ministry, based on O'Meara's work, to describe what is in fact happening in ministry and to argue for it as a norm for the community.[16] The inner circle represents leadership of communities, including bishops and presbyters but also pastoral coordinators, who may be deacons or lay ecclesial ministers, those who preside over the whole community, which includes identifying and coordinating all ministries. The second circle consists of ministers who are prepared and recognized by the church to lead some aspect of ministry. Most often, but not in all cases, these ministers work full-time and are professionally educated. They lead ministries in the areas such as liturgy and worship, pastoral care, catechesis and evangelization, and administration. They work in collaboration with and by the direction of the leader of the community; an important distinction between these first two levels is that leaders of the community preside over the entire community, and leaders of ministries tend not to have this role and authority.

On the third level of the circle, are people who participate in part-time or occasional ministries, perhaps at "varied intensity during stages of life," and have some level of preparation for their ministry; for example a person who serves as a lector, on a youth ministry team, or visits the sick as part of a pastoral care ministry, are all serving as ministers in a designated role, even though they may be occasional (once a week). When disciples are called to serve as ministers in these ways the call maintains the same levels of discernment, preparation, and recognition that Gaillardetz outlines. As in many cases today, congregations and parishes prepare and educate people for their ministries and install or commission them in public prayer and ritual. For O'Meara, "Diversity is to be grounded in the reality of the ministry and church's life. There is considerable difference in preparation and responsibility between the public entry into an episcopal ministry of leadership for the entire dio-

---

[16] Edward Hahnenberg, *Ministries: A Relational Approach* (New York: Crossroad, 2003), 183.

cese and that of a reader at Sunday mass. Nevertheless, the identity of both, bishop and reader, is ministerial."[17] The outer circle that encompasses all the levels represents the baptized people of God.

Hahnenberg states that a "particular minister's place within these concentric circles reflects the minister's place in the church—his or her *ecclesial position*."[18] Three factors determine the ecclesial relationship of a minister to the church and other ministers: "the minister's commitment to ministry," "the significance and public nature of the ministry itself, and the recognition accorded by the community and its leaders."[19] Discerning a vocation to ministry includes discernment of one's ecclesial position within a diversity of ministerial roles.

This long definition of ministry and the explanation of each of its parts help to identify and describe what is essential to the vocation of ministry: leadership, practice, mission, representation, ecclesial recognition, and sacramental blessing. But ministry is not an end in itself and it does not exist for its own purposes. The call to ministry is a distinct vocation insofar as ministers are called to be stewards of discipleship, to be concerned about the whole of discipleship for the sake of the community. Stewardship of disciples requires recognition of the demands of discipleship, especially in its concrete, local, and particular contexts. Ministers commit to a vigilant watchfulness of discipleship with an eye to its full character, vast limitations, and pressing claims. Ministry exists as a service to discipleship for the sake of the church's mission.

In the next chapter we turn to consider how ministry is rooted in the "two hands" of Christ and the Spirit. The practices of ministry, rooted in Jesus' life and ministry, have existed continually throughout history because the Spirit ensures continuity with Jesus and the early church. The Spirit unites disciples through a diversity of charisms in order that the community's life and witness might shine forth and transform the world. The Spirit's charisms for the practices of ministry are given to some who are called to lead disciples in that service.

---

[17] O'Meara, *Theology of Ministry*, 185.
[18] Hahnenberg, *Ministries*, 128.
[19] Ibid., 131.

Sources for Further Reading

Barlett, David L. *Ministry in the New Testament*. Minneapolis: Fortress Press, 1993.

Collins, John N. *Are All Christians Ministers?* Collegeville, MN: Liturgical Press, 1992.

———. *Diakonia: Re-interpreting the Ancient Sources*. New York: Oxford University Press, 1990.

Congar, Yves. *Lay People in the Church*. Translated by Donald Attwater. Westminster, MD: Newman Press, 1965.

Gregorios, Paulos Mar. *The Meaning and Nature of Diakonia*. Geneva: WCC Publications, 1988.

Hahnenberg, Edward P. *Ministries: A Relational Approach*. New York: Crossroad, 2003.

McBrien, Richard P. *Ministry: A Theological, Pastoral Handbook*. San Francisco, CA: Harper and Row, 1987.

Mitchell, Nathan. *Mission and Ministry: History and Theology in the Sacrament of Order*. Wilmington, DE: Michael Glazier Inc., 1982.

O'Meara, Thomas F. *A Theology of Ministry*. Rev. ed. Mahwah, NJ: Paulist Press, 1999.

Osborne, Kenan B. *Orders and Ministry*. Maryknoll, NY: Orbis Books, 2006.

Schillebeeckx, Edward. *Ministry: Leadership in the Community of Jesus Christ*. New York: Crossroad, 1981.

———. *The Church with a Human Face: A New and Expanded Theology of Ministry*. New York: Crossroad, 1985.

Wood, Susan K. *Sacramental Orders*. Collegeville, MN: Liturgical Press, 2000.

———, ed. *Ordering the Baptismal Priesthood*. Collegeville, MN: Liturgical Press, 2003.

World Council of Churches. *Baptism, Eucharist and Ministry*. Faith and Order Paper No. 111, 1982.

Zizioulas, John. *Being as Communion: Studies in Personhood and the Church*. Crestwood, NY: St. Vladimir's Seminary Press, 1985.

Chapter 4

Jesus and the Spirit's Charisms in
Relationship to the
Six Practices of Ministry

As I discussed in chapter 1, Jesus is the foundation for the practice of discipleship. He exemplifies what it means to be a follower, witness, worshiper, neighbor, forgiver, prophet, and steward in his actions and identity. Jesus expresses in what he does who he is. We could say that his vocation, the service he offers in the world, is integrated into who he is and how he lives. His vocation rests on one purpose: to draw people into communion with divine mystery and life. Jesus' life and relationships become the pattern for disciples and their vocations. Discipleship is the first call to follow Jesus and in each and every vocation the call to discipleship is manifest. It is in and through vocation that discipleship is lived.

Jesus is also minister and his ministry is the foundation for the practices of ministry. We find the six practices of ministry exemplified in his actions and speech, and continued by the early apostles and first ministers as the foundation of the church. In the Jewish tradition of Jesus' time, he was recognized as a teacher, preacher, healer, and prophet. He is not identified as presider of worship or administrator, mostly because he does not serve as a priest in the temple, nor does he belong to the Pharisees or Sadducees, leaders of the Jewish community that oversaw the laws, organization, and well-being of the community. His lineage and ministry identify him primarily within the prophetic tradition. But worship and administration have an important foundation in his ministry and in the early community, certainly in the ministries of Peter and Paul and the first generation. Thus, we can look to Jesus' ministry and the early followers as the foundation for the six practices of ministry. This is the Christological foundation of ministry.

But I have also claimed a pneumatological dimension to ministry through the idea of the Spirit's charisms. What are the charisms for these practices? In this chapter I identify three charisms for each practice. One charism relates to being, the kind of person I am; this charism might also be called virtue because it points to the dispositions and habits to do the good. For example, if I practice patience with things that irritate me, over time I will become a patient person. The second relates to knowing, to the kinds of knowledge that are important to learn about discipleship and ministry if one is to lead the community in its mission. The third charism points to doing, to skill and competence in action, to how I intentionally embody in what I say and do an act that aims toward the flourishing of discipleship. I fully recognize that the Spirit's gifts for each practice are not limited to three, and I invite the reader to expand on this list and develop it further. I have identified these three aspects of the self—being, knowing, and doing—as core features of a practice, which will be introduced and discussed in chapters 5 and 6. In this chapter I want to define the six practices of ministry, their Christological and pneumatological foundation, as well as charisms related to being, knowing, and doing.

The Ministry of Teaching

Jesus is teacher. Jesus is readily identified in the gospel stories as a great teacher. Though he is distinct from other types of teachers, he nonetheless embodies some aspects of teaching common for his time. For instance, he is recognized as teaching as "one having authority, and not as the scribes" (Mark 1:22) even though he does not seem to have formal training as a scholar of the law, such as a scribe or Pharisee. Like sages or cynic philosophers (groups to whom many scholars compare Jesus), Jesus does not seem to establish a school but rather moves around as an itinerant rabbi, teaching common people, through a variety of means, about who he understands God to be. As a Jewish teacher, Jesus has learned the Scriptures of his community and through study, prayer, and his experience of Yahweh, launches a ministry of teaching that both challenges rigid and narrow interpretations of the law and draws out radical claims about God's love and mercy. People address Jesus as "rabbi," which was not an official title but one of respect and honor, a recognition that Jesus taught "the way of God in accordance with truth" (Mark 12:14).

Jesus teaches in two primary ways. The first is through his use of language and words. The second is through the embodiment of his teachings in his actions, most notably table fellowship. In examining Jesus' use of language, we find that he teaches using a variety of oral communication: one-line riddles, allegories, hyperbole, stories, and parables. Jesus is especially noteworthy in his teaching of parables, which are stories aimed to teach a religious or moral insight. Recognized as an extended metaphor, parables are meant to draw two different ideas or images together in order to draw out a third idea. In most of Jesus' parables, the reign of God is being compared to an ordinary thing, such as a mustard seed, and this comparison is meant to awaken the listener to understand something about God's relationship to us. Rather than lecturing about who God is and what God is doing in relationship to humanity and creation, parables were a way that Jesus could make his point in story form, oftentimes in a surprising and startling way, about what God is like. Because these images and stories are contextual, drawn from the Jewish culture of his time, contemporary listeners may not always understand the element of shock and surprise contained in the "punch line" of a parable: the Samaritan is the one who cares; the father offers unconditional love and forgiveness to the wayward son; the foreman of the vineyard has an unusual sense of justice. The parables also show that God's presence is alive in the here and now, though as imperceptible as yeast or as tiny as a mustard seed, the "reigning" power of God's mercy is enlivening and bursting forth in astonishing abundance. Parables are meant to have a shock value, to surprise us, and to leave a sense of openness to how the hearer will respond: they may anger or convert the listener, but they are not meant to leave a person neutral about their moral choices. For example, in Luke's famous parable of the prodigal son, Jesus leaves his listener with a question: does the older brother attend the celebration or not?

Jesus also teaches by doing. He embodies his teaching in his life and witness. If the father forgives the prodigal son with an open heart and warm embrace, then disciples are meant to embrace the sinner and outcast as our brother, sister, and friend. Jesus demonstrates this radical teaching most often at table in which he enters the "praxis of inclusive wholeness."[1] Jesus demonstrates to his hosts that he is willing to eat with anyone: rich and poor (Luke 5:27-39; Mark 1:31), family and friends as well as religious leaders (Luke 14:1-24; 10:38-42), and Jews, Gentiles, and Samaritans (Luke 11:37-54; Mark 8:1-9; and John 4:4-42). Clearly, Jesus did not follow the table etiquette of his time and, through his own practices of table fellowship, breaks down the religious purity laws and gender barriers that clearly kept people from being together. Jesus' table fellowship practices with sinners and the unclean (Luke 7:36-50; 19:1-10), probably more than his teachings in words, did more to bring about hatred and enmity toward him: many of his followers, as well as religious leaders, could not tolerate this inclusive practice. As Robert Karris states, "Jesus got himself crucified by the way he ate."[2] Like the parables, Jesus' table fellowship calls us to determine who we will eat with and what kind of hospitality we are willing to practice at table.

The ministry of teaching consists of a variety of activities, including evangelization, catechesis, and theology. To evangelize means to draw people to the faith, to arouse a desire to learn more about Christ, and to begin the journey of conversion on the path of discipleship. Catechesis comes from the Greek verb *katechein*, which means to resound or echo, sounding down and reechoing to another. Catechesis is a form of instruction and learning that is meant to make a disciple's faith conscious, thoughtful, and active. In the New Testament, the verb is used to mean "instruction in the way of the Lord" or "instruction given by word of mouth" (Luke 1:4; Acts 18:25; 1 Cor 14:19; Gal 6:6). Like Jesus, Paul understood the ministry of teaching as oral instruction, a handing on of all that had been received.

Theology is, in St. Anselm's famous phrase, "faith seeking understanding." As study or talk about God, theology engages reflection, reasoning, and understanding about the central claims of Christian faith. According to Roger Haight, "theology is a discipline that interprets all reality—human existence, society, history, the world, and God—in terms of the symbols of the Christian faith."[3] Theology is also "understanding seeking faith." It brings questions from the faith tradition to human realities, but it also brings insights and questions from life to the religious claims of the Christian community. The work of articulating the substance of the faith as well as the forms through which to communicate

[1] Elisabeth Schüssler Fiorenza, *In Memory of Her: A Feminist Theological Reconstruction of Christian Origins* (New York: Crossroad, 1983), 119.

[2] Robert Karris, *Luke: Artist and Theologian* (New York: Paulist Press, 1985), 47.

[3] Roger Haight, *Dynamics of Theology* (Mahwah, NJ: Paulist Press, 1990), 216.

the message has traditionally been part of the teaching office of the church. According to Richard Osmer, the "teaching office" has included three tasks: to determine the church's normative beliefs and practices, to interpret belief and practice in cultural and historical contexts, and to create and sustain educational institutions, processes, and curricula for teaching and learning.[4]

Drawing from Jesus' practice and the practice of excellent teachers through the ages, the Spirit grants (at least) three charisms for the practice of teaching ministry: knowledge and understanding (knowing), effective use of language in speech and writing (doing), and humility (being).

Teachers are given the gift of knowledge about, as well as understanding in, the way of Christ, the Christian faith, and the tradition. To have knowledge about Christ and the way of discipleship, the minister is called, as Thomas Groome says, to "engage life with thoughtful comprehension, to construct an intelligible world for ourselves and to appropriate some measure of meaning and value from it. In concert with our bodies, and moved by our wills, our minds function to perceive and recognize, to understand and comprehend, to discern and judge, and, prompting our physical agency and will, to decide and choose about ourselves and the world around us."[5] To have the gift of knowledge is to know human reality, the whole self of mind as well as the heart; it also means understanding the created world, the cosmos and the natural world, as well as politics, society, and culture through history as well as in contemporary situations.

Parker Palmer, in his reflections on teaching, notes that we can seek three types of knowledge: pure, speculative knowledge; knowledge as a means to practical ends; and knowledge arising from love.[6] Each kind of knowing has a role in teaching and learning, and each has a drawback or danger. Pure, speculative knowledge runs the danger of rendering people or things as "objects," disconnected from our relationship to them or any communal foundation. I can study the Scriptures and seek to know their historical, political, and social setting as a cultural artifact— something I can know about, but not in relationship to myself or a community. Or I can seek to obtain knowledge about the Scripture in order

---

[4] Richard Robert Osmer, *A Teachable Spirit: Recovering the Teaching Office of the Church* (Louisville, KY: Westminster/John Knox Press, 1990), 15.

[5] Thomas H. Groome, *Sharing Faith: A Comprehensive Approach to Religious Education and Pastoral Ministry* (San Francisco, CA: Harper, 1991), 88.

[6] Parker J. Palmer, *To Know as We Are Known: A Spirituality of Education* (San Francisco, CA: Harper & Row, 1983), 6–8.

to preach the gospel effectively to the community in order to enhance their knowledge and love of Christ. I can also study the Scriptures and understand the various theories, discussions, and arguments about their meaning and context because I love the Scriptures and I stand within a community of teaching and learning the ways of life embraced within the biblical text. Knowledge about and knowledge for are not necessarily an obstacle to knowledge from love, and in fact they are necessary for ministers to become teachers of the faith. Because knowledge is power, it is necessary to discern for what purpose we seek knowledge, which is a paramount question for teachers. Palmer writes that "the act of knowing is an act of love, the act of entering and embracing the reality of the other, of allowing the other to enter and embrace our own. In such knowing we know and are known as members of one community, and our knowing becomes a way of reweaving that community's bonds."[7]

A second charism for teaching is the gift to invite and instruct people in the way of discipleship through oral and written expression as well as a life lived in the ways of discipleship. To be an effective teacher is to have the charisms for communicating knowledge about, for, and in relationship to Christ and the tradition. Teachers must develop forms of oral speech that can help people to understand. We commonly associate teaching with schooling and lecture, leading discussion, and explaining concepts. These are important gifts to develop for particular contexts of teaching. But like Jesus, ministers receive a wide range of gifts and capacities to use language through metaphor, story, and parable to help awaken people to the reality of who God is and how God is present in their lives. In addition to effective speech, ministers learn to use image, music, silence, literature—all the various forms of language and communication in a culture that can express religious meaning and truth.

Teachers do not merely impart knowledge about the faith, but create an environment of learning that promotes discipleship. The charism to teach includes attention and commitment to ways in which people can learn the faith. Thomas Groome identifies seven commitments for a way of teaching the life of faith: to engage learners in actively participating; to attend and pay attention to learners as they experience, know, and initiate; to allow learners to express thoughts, feelings, and action; to initiate reflection on what is learned; to invite critical assessment and

---

[7] Ibid., 8.

questioning; to access the tradition; and to foster appropriation, judgment, and decision about what learners know, understand, and believe.[8]

A third charism for teaching is the moral virtue and disposition of humility. From the Greek word *humilis*, humility means "from the earth." Humility is the virtue of having the right perspective of oneself, neither too low and self-degrading or too high and full of pride. Humility is knowing that one is dust "from the earth" as well as created in the image of God, and holding this reality in creative and truthful tension. In relationship to teaching, humility is the recognition that what one knows and one's capacity to communicate it effectively to others is rooted in the Spirit's gifts and that the right and proper use of these gifts has been granted in order that disciples might learn the ways of God. It is not to obtain knowledge for the sake of merely knowing about or for using knowledge for self-advancement. Humility is knowing what I do not know, realizing what I cannot know, and accepting the ways of God as finally a mystery I cannot fully comprehend. Humility teaches that knowledge is not something to be consumed or grasped at, a means of gaining power or control over others, or a path to self-righteousness. Rather, humility is the practice of embracing an identity as a learner, a follower, in relationship to all that we can and cannot know.

The Ministry of Preaching

In addition to being a well-known and provocative teacher, Jesus is also preacher. His preaching ministry identifies him within the prophetic tradition; he is called to speak and exhort his listeners to heed the commands of Yahweh and reform their lives. Many of his listeners identify him as prophet, including Herod Antipas's court who call him "one of the prophets of old" (Mark 6:15; Luke 9:8), Simon the Pharisee (Luke 7:39), and the Roman authorities (Matt 21:46). Luke calls Jesus a "prophet mighty in deed and word" (Luke 24:19b). And some reactions to Jesus point out that being a prophet was not without its problems, for when he is rejected at Nazareth, he states that "prophets are not without honor, except in their hometown, and among their own kin, and in their own house" (Mark 6:4; Matt 13:57; Luke 4:24). Of course John the Baptist was

---

[8] Thomas Groome, *Educating for Life: A Spiritual Vision for Every Teacher and Parent* (Allen, TX: Thomas More, 1998), 430–39.

winning a reputation as a dangerous prophet, one who was calling for repentance and a radical change of life, a message that was too threatening for some.

Jesus is connected with several strands of the prophetic tradition beginning with Moses. Like the great prophet Moses, Jesus stands among the people interpreting God's will and justice through Torah. As noted above, he is not a trained scribe and is not interested in legal disputes regarding Torah. Rather, Jesus is guided by his reading of the Torah together with his experience of God's love. He is drawn toward the prophets' claim of Yahweh's love for the sinner and outcast and a desire for justice for the oppressed. While Jesus does preach about conversion and judgment, he is not drawn to the prophets' focus on a wrathful God who seeks vengeance and destruction. Jesus' prophetic message called for people to make a decision, to live according to Yahweh's ways or to face destruction that comes from rejecting that path. Whatever he thought of the "end time," Jesus believes the moment of decision is now and radical conversion of heart and behavior must commence. And Jesus does not seem to think that God's reigning presence was only a future eschatological reality; he seemed convinced that God's love and justice were in the here and now, but not to be gained by extreme observance of religious law, such as the Essenes practiced, or by social revolution and war, as some Zealots advocated. As prophet, Jesus preached to his own people about a radically different worldview from within their own tradition, yet deeply at odds with other prophetic and religious messages.

Preaching, as it developed in the early Christian tradition, is the proclamation of the good news of salvation through Jesus. The Greek words for preaching in the New Testament include *kerussein*, to herald, proclaim; *evangelizesthai*, to announce the gospel; and *marturein*, to witness. Preaching has taken place in a wide variety of contexts, including street corners, but worship and liturgy have been the most common setting for the practice of Christian preaching. Preaching is a public act, a dialogical event between the preacher and the listeners.

The basic act of preaching, according to Thomas Long, is to bear witness to the gospel on behalf of the community. In many instances this means interpreting the written gospel, the Scriptures, for the sake of the community's life together. In this context, the charisms of preaching include knowledge of and the capacity to interpret the Word of God, the ability to speak persuasively to the people, and the virtues of empathy and truth-telling.

Preaching in the context of worship involves interpreting the biblical message for the community. Like teaching, knowledge about the Bible is not enough to be an effective preacher. As Long notes, the preacher is not merely gathering information about the text. The preacher "is listening for a voice, looking for a presence, hoping for the claim of God to be encountered through the text."[9] The preacher is sent on behalf of the congregation to listen to God's voice in the Scripture and to bear witness about this truth for this community. In other words, "it is not the preacher who goes to the scripture; it is the church that goes to the scripture by means of the preacher. The preacher is a member of the community, set apart by them and sent to the scripture to search, to study, and to listen obediently on their behalf."[10] To interpret the Word for the community requires study and exegesis of the Scripture, that includes appreciation for the cultural and social setting of the text as well as the tradition of interpretation about texts. Interpretation of texts is motivated by knowledge in love with the biblical text, even with its complexity, ambiguity, distance, and biases.

The preacher's knowledge of Scripture, and capacity to exegete and interpret texts well, is closely tied to the virtue of empathy and truth-telling. Empathy points to the gift of understanding and experiencing the feelings, thoughts, ideas, and circumstances of the hearer. The preacher does not speak about the biblical text as something from the past, but as the living word proclaimed in the present, in this time and place for this community. Long writes, "when preachers go to the scripture, then, they must take the people with them, since what will be heard there is a word for them."[11] Preaching requires the gifts for listening closely to the community, its joys and pain, its questions and its sins.

As a witness on behalf of the community, preaching requires telling the truth, both about what the preacher witnesses in the text as well as in the community. As with any prophetic task, the gift of truth-telling is both liberating and painful. To listen for God's word, the preacher may find answers to people's deepest questions and longings, but the Scriptures may also "call those questions into question. The truth found there may resolve a problem, and then again it may deepen that problem."[12]

[9] Thomas G. Long, *The Witness of Preaching* (Louisville, KY: Westminster/John Knox Press, 1989), 44.

[10] Ibid., 45.

[11] Ibid.

[12] Ibid.

The message the preacher seeks is far from simple and easy: it both heals and judges disciples.

A third charism is the gift of speaking persuasively in order that people are able to hear, listen, encounter, and decide about God's Word in their lives. Preachers prepare sermons and deliver sermons. The charism of speaking persuasively before the community is its own capacity and skill, often referred to as rhetoric or persuasive speech. Ministers can hone their abilities in biblical exegesis and understand the people's situation but fail to communicate in words the message they believe can draw the listener to think, feel, and act. Preaching is rhetorical speech, persuasive in its intention, and must be delivered in ways that it can be heard, understood, and considered by the listener. Like teachers, preachers develop different styles for communicating, and we sometimes confuse a bold, flashy style with the charism. But the charism of preaching comes in many different styles and forms, and the gift is manifest in terms of "oral competence," which includes learning effective patterns of "speech production, audibility, breath control, volume, emotion, voice, tonality, articulation, pacing, rate, and presence."[13] Interpreting the Word, understanding the people, drawing the two together, and speaking a clear and compelling message to the situation are essential charisms of preaching.

The Ministry of Care

Jesus is healer. As Jesus' table fellowship is his teaching in action, we could say that Jesus' preaching in action is healing. The healing stories constitute a major theme of the gospel writers and in Mark's gospel nearly half of the stories of Jesus' public ministry are miracles of healing. The link between Jesus' preaching and the healing miracles is the powerful message that God loves each person and intends their full wholeness in mind, body, and spirit. This loving, healing presence is not only an eschatological promise, a future, otherworldly reality, but a promise that can be known and experienced in the present through the healing of the mind and body and the forgiveness of sins.

Jesus informs his followers of the types of healings they have witnessed, recalling the prophet Isaiah's vision: "Go and tell John what you

[13] Teresa Fry Brown, "Voice and Diction," in *Teaching Preaching as a Christian Practice*, ed. Thomas G. Long and Leonora Tubbs Tisdale (Louisville, KY: Westminster John Knox Press, 2008), 180.

hear and see: the blind receive their sight, the lame walk, the lepers are cleansed, the deaf hear, the dead are raised, and the poor have the good news brought to them" (Matt 11:4-5; Isa 35:5-6; 29:18-19). Jesus is not a physician, nor is he recognized as one. The woman who touches his cloak has, in fact, "endured much under many physicians, and had spent all that she had" (Mark 5:26), which shows that medical remedies were widely available from physicians. But Jesus does not offer a cure through a remedy. Nor is the category of "miracle" or "miracle worker" ascribed to Jesus. The most common term refers to these events as *dunameis* or "dynamic" acts of power. Jesus does not enact this power to prove who he is or to attract a crowd; in fact, he warns people not to tell of their healing, perhaps because he did not want the act or himself to be misinterpreted.

The deed is consistent with the message: the healing stories point to God's presence as healer, redeemer, consoler, and restorer of life. God intends that sickness, suffering, and death will not be the final word or reality for each human person, but that healing from all misery will come about in the final days. In this sense the healings are a sign, a glimpse of the eschaton breaking in the present moment. Jesus did not heal all the sick or bring back to life all the dead he encountered, nor did he end sickness and death as human realities. The healings point to God's loving care in the midst of present suffering and an eschatological future in which all suffering and evil is overcome. In this regard, Christ's resurrection is consistent with Jesus' healing ministry, for his new life points to God's intention that death is not the end of human existence.

If this was the sole purpose of the healings, Jesus might not have met with such outright rejection by some. For instance after healing a man, the Pharisees "went out and conspired against [Jesus], how to destroy him" (Matt 12:14). The fact that Jesus is a healer is not the threat in his community, for there were other healers in his time, and some prophets, such as Elijah and Elisha, were known to be healers. Rather, the healing stories point to two difficulties. First, Jesus breaks religious laws and taboos by touching the sick and thereby transgresses the barriers of exclusion marking the sick as an outcast. Second, along with healing the physical ailments of some people, he also forgives their sins, so that physical, spiritual, and moral healing are one act, but this also transgresses the religious belief that illness is caused by sin. Perhaps more than anything, healing as restoring the physical and moral status of the person, raises questions about Jesus' authority and power.

The tradition of care derives from the biblical image of "shepherd" and refers to the concern for persons in trouble or distress. The ministry of care, or pastoral care, has traditionally included four aspects: healing, sustaining, guiding, and reconciling.[14] These practices take place with persons, groups, and communities; care at its best is rooted in and facilitated by community, even when it is practiced one-on-one. Healing generally refers to helping a person, group, or community "overcome some impairment by restoring" them to "wholeness" and "leading them" to advance beyond a previous condition.[15] The gospel healing stories often address physical illness and disease, but the ministry of pastoral care generally does not aim to heal physical problems as much as it aims to heal the vulnerability evoked by illness and to draw a person to a new level of spiritual insight, trust, and peace. Caregiving often means helping those who live with physical ailments, disease, and pain to find meaning, release, and hope in the midst of illness and to celebrate and live in gratitude when illnesses are healed.

Sustaining refers to accompanying those who experience loss, which includes, according to William Clebsch and Charles Jaekle, the tasks of preservation (addressing fears and threats), consolation (assuring the person's value and dignity in the community), consolidation (mobilizing persons to understand their suffering in relationship to a larger worldview), and redemption (guiding a person in rebuilding his or her life). The third aspect of care, guiding, is the practice of helping persons and communities in moral discernment: what ought I or we to do? Reconciliation refers to the practice of helping persons and communities in the art of forgiving one another as well as themselves and to restore relationships with God and neighbor.[16]

Pastoral care today is defined in the *New Dictionary of Pastoral Studies* as "those activities of the Church which are directed towards maintaining or restoring the health and wholeness of individuals and communities in the context of God's redemptive purposes for all creation." Care encompasses a broad range of activities including offering skilled advice, counseling, performing healing rituals and sacraments, charitable work and social action, and simple acts of comfort, support, and encouragement. As Jeanne Stevenson-Moessner states, "pastoral care is an outreach of compassion often accompanied by an action of care. That action can be as ordinary as offering food to someone who is isolated and lonely

---

[14] William A. Clebsch and Charles R. Jaekle, *Pastoral Care in Historical Perspective* (New York: Harper Torchbooks, 1967).

[15] Ibid., 8.

[16] Ibid., 32–66.

or as complicated as intervening in a medical crisis."[17] Pastoral care encompasses a variety of competences and is practiced in a wide range of settings, beginning in the home, congregation, and neighborhood, and including hospitals, schools, residential care facilities, prisons, and hospices. The charisms for the ministry of pastoral care include the virtue of compassion, the ability to guide, sustain, and facilitate healing and reconciliation, and knowledge about the dynamics of sin, suffering, and grief as well as forgiveness, healing, and joy.

The first charism of pastoral care is compassion for the suffering and well-being of another person. Compassion refers to the ability to "suffer with" another, to recognize the basic human experiences of another's story and experience. The biblical terms compassion, mercy, and pity point to an inner feeling related to "cherishing," "soothing," "tenderness," a "gentle attitude," and deep attachment to another, especially in distress. Interestingly, compassion is a feeling or a response rooted in the body, related to the womb, loins, and bowels, pointing to one of the deepest connections of a mother and child, the place of deep love. Mercy is a characteristic attributed to God, related to God's righteousness, justice, and love (Hos 2:19), but it is also a demand placed on those God calls. It is required toward family and neighbor, as well orphans, the aged, the poor, and the widow (Ps 72:13; Ezek 16:5). The gospel writers note that Jesus is compassionate, moved to pity, filled with sorrow and mercy for the distressed, recognizing them as sheep without a shepherd (Matt 9:36; 14:14; 20:34; Mark 1:41; 6:34; 8:2; Luke 7:13). The gift of mercy and compassion is the source of reaching out to care for another in need.

Another charism of care is the ability to guide, direct, assist, and facilitate healing and reconciliation. A core charism in relationship to all aspects of care is the ability to actively engage in another person's situation, which involves both active listening and discerned response. Active listening to our own soul and to the souls of others, according to Jean Stairs, is "more central to life than anything else we do." It involves "essential skills normally identified with the act of listening, such as expressing interest by caring behavior, using appropriate facial expressions and posture, posing open-ended questions, closely observing nonverbal clues, responding by paraphrasing, clarifying, supporting, probing, understanding, confronting, evaluating, and recommending."

---

[17] Jeanne Stevenson-Moessner, *A Primer in Pastoral Care* (Minneapolis: Fortress Press, 2005), 17.

Such intentional listening requires "a definite spirit and intentionality" since "we are listening for the very voice, presence, or absence of God in the soul, the core of our lives where meaning is created."[18] The charism of active listening, for Stairs, includes intentionality, obedience, intimacy, receptivity, hospitality, and focus. The gift is the capacity to open one's self to another and to encounter the person as one to be known and understood.

Augustine noted that the care of souls is "preaching in private." The caregiver also is an active responder, which involves discerning words of comfort or challenge, questions to ask, as well as waiting in silence. To offer guidance and to facilitate healing and reconciliation requires the caregiver to speak and embody the gospel message of God's mercy and compassion in ways that will help a disciple understand their situation and choose to live more faithfully within it. Active listening and responding is based on the conviction that God is present as the caregiver of creation. The ministry of caring presence means "being aware" of a threefold relationality: God's presence in the other person or community, the uniqueness of each person and situation, and one's self as representative of the good shepherd.[19]

Because the practice of pastoral care requires ministers to stand close to and accompany people in some of the most profound human encounters with life and death, the Spirit blesses them with the charism of knowing and understanding the human condition: human frailty that is wrought by sin and destruction, or by illness and disease, or by loss and pain. It also requires learning and knowing the dynamics of healing, the ways of reconciliation with self, God, and neighbor. Pastoral care requires a theological view of injustice, suffering, and pain: human conditions that cry out for a response from disciples who seek to embody the compassion of God for their neighbor.

The Ministry of Prayer and Worship

Jesus leads prayer and worship. He is readily identified as teacher, preacher, and healer, though he is not a temple priest. Within first-century Judaism, temple worship was the predominant form of worship, and

---

[18] Jean Stairs, *Listening for the Soul: Pastoral Care and Spiritual Direction* (Minneapolis, MN: Fortress Press, 2000), 17.

[19] John Patton, *Pastoral Care: An Essential Guide* (Nashville, TN: Abingdon Press, 2005), 22.

Jesus was not a priest in the temple for the simple reason that he did not come from the family of Levites who served as priests. In fact, we learn from the infancy narratives that Jesus belongs to the house of David, a royal but not a priestly family.

Jesus seems to have a complicated relationship to temple worship and its priests. On the one hand, he is an observant Jew and participates in temple worship. At least twice, once as a young boy and later as an adult, he makes his way to Jerusalem to attend the celebrations of Passover, and of course the second trip leads to his execution (Luke 2:41-51; 22:7-8). In the healing stories, Jesus tells the ten lepers to go and show themselves to the priests and observe the religious law that allows a person healed from leprosy to come back into the community (Luke 17:11-14). And on the night before he dies, with his friends gathered around, he observes the Passover meal, following the rituals and prayers repeated for hundreds of years.

In addition to worshiping as an observant Jew, however, Jesus is quite critical of temple worship, particularly rigid interpretations of purity laws that keep people from gaining "access" to the divine. In one of the most shocking scenes in the gospel stories, Jesus is angry and violently sweeps aside the vendor's tables in the temple (Matt 21:12-17; Mark 11:15-19; Luke 19:45-48; John 2:13-22). The very idea that God's love or favor could be bought through animal sacrifice infuriates him. His radical act recalls the prophet's same critique hundreds of years before: Yahweh does not require blood sacrifice but a clean heart (Ps 51:10-17).

Based on the gospel stories, we can see in Jesus' ministry the foundation of worship as an integral aspect of the life of discipleship, and in the early church we see the necessity of calling forth worship leaders as communities are formed and established. How is Jesus the foundation to the ministry of worship? While he is not a temple priest, he leads the disciples in prayer and worship in two important ways. First, he teaches them to pray with the Lord's Prayer (Matt 6:1-15; Luke 11:2-4), and he leads the Passover ritual, offering the traditional prayers of thanksgiving and praise (Matt 26:26-29; Mark 14:22-25; Luke 22:14-23). A new kind of worship emerges, however, when he proclaims the bread and wine his body and blood (John 6:35-59), and washes their feet, all signs of the new covenant God is making with the people through this radical embodiment of servant-love (John 13:1-17).

What is worship and worship leadership? Christian worship is love, devotion, and adoration for God in Christ through the Spirit, demonstrated perhaps best by the healed leper's response to God's mercy: "Then one of them, when he saw that he was healed, turned back, praising

God with a loud voice. He prostrated himself at Jesus' feet and thanked him" (Luke 17:15-16). Worship is a disposition of the heart that is ready to bow down and acknowledge God as God.

Worship entails rites, rituals, sacred stories, songs, symbols, and creeds that express the fundamental claims about who God is and what God has done for the people. "Christian liturgy . . . is the ongoing prayer, proclamation, and life of Jesus Christ—a sacrifice of thanksgiving and praise—offered to God in and through his body in the world. That is, Christian liturgy is our response to the self-giving of God in, with, and through the One who leads us in prayer. The community is called into being to continue that prayer on behalf of the whole world."[20]

The ministry of leading worship entails, in most Christian churches, a range of situations. First is the presiding role at Sunday liturgy, the celebration of sacraments (within or outside Sunday worship such as baptism or confirmation), and other formal liturgical rites (such as funerals and burials). Presiding is a "service of leadership in a common and participatory action called 'liturgy,' therefore an action that with full intent and purpose is done in the presence of God. . . . [I]t normally assumes an already existing relationship with the community assembled."[21]

A second aspect of the ministry of worship is leading prayer outside liturgical settings, for example, at the beginning of a meeting or a class, at the bedside of a sick or dying person, on retreats, before meals and celebrations—any of the daily occurrences where a minister finds her- or himself leading the community in prayer no matter how large the community since "where two or three are gathered in my name, I am there among them" (Matt 18:20).

The three charisms for leading worship span across all the various contexts in which ministers lead worship and prayer. First is the charism of knowledge and wisdom about the tradition's rituals, symbols, rubrics, and prayer forms. No minister can lead worship without understanding what worship is, what the rituals, sacraments, and norms for worship are in the community and tradition that he or she leads, how they have developed over time, and their theological meaning and interpretation. Because worship is a multifaceted form of communication, ministers need a deep and appreciative understanding of the language of worship,

---

[20] Don E. Saliers, *Worship as Theology: Foretaste of Glory Divine* (Nashville, TN: Abingdon Press, 1994), 86.

[21] Robert W. Hovda, *Strong, Loving and Wise: Presiding in Liturgy* (Collegeville, MN: Liturgical Press, 1983), 7–8.

how worship "works" effectively in a given community, and the context of worship in sacred time (liturgical calendars) and space (art and environment).

As noted above, the minister cannot merely have knowledge about worship, but through his or her own worshipful practice, must be wise about leading the community in its practice of worship. The minister must have knowledge about the types of prayer forms in the Christian tradition and how to develop appropriate words for prayer in particular settings: prayers of praising, thanking and blessing, invoking and be-seeching, lamenting, confessing, and interceding. The kind of knowing that gives birth to prayer and worship is born of a "passional knowing—a process of being formed in specific affections and dispositions in the way we live that manifests what is known about God."[22]

Worship is prayer enacted; we "do this in memory of" Jesus' actions at the Last Supper. Worship is about enacting the story again and again, allowing the narrative to be scripted onto our lives. From Pentecostal revivals to the monastic Liturgy of the Hours, Christian worshipers enact ritual gestures and words. The second charism of leading worship and prayer is the gift for embodied speech and gesture that communicate sacred story and realities among the worshiping community. In other words, the minister has an embodied presence that is meant to lead worshipers in the embodied ritual of worship; the minister is not the only one worshiping, gesturing, or speaking. As Aidan Kavanagh writes, "the minister, especially the one who presides, should know both the assembly and its liturgy so well that his looks, words, and gestures have a confident and easy grace about them. He presides not over the assembly but within it; he does not lead it but serves it; he is the speaker of its house of worship . . . steeped in reverent pastoral responsibility that is completely infused with the assembly and its tradition of liturgical worship."[23]

The third charism is the gift of adoration that invites participation by the community in loving response to God. Ministers can read words from a book, recite a memorized prayer, and pray spontaneously, but it is not so much the form of the prayer that matters but the kind of pres-ence that the minister presents and evokes in speaking the words truly and with a spirit of adoration. As in preaching, the presider is praying

---

[22] Saliers, *Worship as Theology*, 86.

[23] Aidan Kavanagh, *Elements of Rite: A Handbook of Liturgical Style* (New York: Pueblo Publishing Co., 1982), 13.

on behalf of the community, bringing forward the community's prayers—its hopes and longings—before God. The charism for presiding at worship is one of adoration for God along with the other charisms of empathy, compassion, and understanding of the people whose prayer is being lifted up to God. This feeling, combined with one's own sense of awe and gratitude to God, enables the presider, even within their personal limitations, to lead the assembly in divine worship. "Along with this sense of human limits, a feeling and attitude of reverence, a sense of mystery and of the fact that the action in which the assembly is engaging is a mystery—this feeling and sense is indispensable and inimitable. . . . People must be enabled to experience in the presider's posture, gestures, movements, words this intangible and essential feeling. . . . [I]t is the faith sense of the people being the whole Christ, of church as the body of the Lord."[24] Because ministers represent a community, public vocal prayer is not the individual prayer of a minister but rather the gift for naming, identifying, and speaking the prayer of the community. The charism of adoration is the gift of calling forward the Body of Christ into communion and community for its mission in the world.

The Ministry of Social Mercy and Justice

We see in Jesus' ministry the foundation for ministries of mercy and justice. He teaches, by word and example, about God's love for the lowly, poor, and outcast. He preaches a message of radical love and forgiveness that neighbors are to extend to each other, as God has extended to them. And he heals those who are sick, shunned, and deemed unclean, inviting them into a new fellowship of community without barriers. Because he worships Yahweh with his whole self, he is able to bend down and wash the feet of his disciples, becoming like a slave in rendering service. In all these ways, Jesus' ministry is the foundation for ministries of mercy and justice.

Who are the poor that Jesus ministers to and why? Is not Jesus' message and ministry inclusive of all persons? Does he not tell his disciples "You always have the poor with you" (Mark 14:7)? The category "the poor" in the Scriptures has two basic references. First, it generally refers to persons who are economically deprived in some way, who do not have enough material means to live, either a lack of money, food, shelter,

---

[24] Hovda, *Strong, Loving and Wise*, 67.

or clothing. They lack the basic sustenance to survive, and in the world of Jesus' time, this meant becoming a beggar or being dependent on family or kin if they would accept you. The second reference to "the poor" is more general and it serves as a synonym for the needy, weak, afflicted, oppressed, humbled, naked, orphan, widow, or sojourner. All of these designations may be due to economic poverty, but they also stem from other conditions such as illness and disease, slavery, gender restrictions, inheritance laws, ethnicity, and religious purity laws. Illness and disease were often seen as signs of sin and failure, a judgment by God against the person. The sin deemed the person an outcast, unworthy to approach the community or temple, but also in the case of contagious diseases such as leprosy, it made a person an outcast from the normal patterns of everyday life. Being a slave meant that a person was property, owned and possessed by another, and used as a means of labor and service. Women lived under a set of prescribed social and religious norms that did not allow them to inherit money or property. They were allowed into the first level of the temple but could never approach the holy of holies because of purity laws. People such as Samaritans were considered ethnically unworthy and hence unclean.

In each of these examples, "poor" represents deprivation in many forms, from basic physical needs to basic human dignity. The injustice, in Jesus' eyes, is the social practices and norms that determine a person unworthy to be treated as neighbor, a child of God, *imago Dei*. He opposes the barriers that the community puts around a person, barriers to their full humanity, to relationships within the community, and to the divine. There is, however, only one barrier to full communion with God and neighbor, according to Jesus, and he spells it out clearly in Matthew 25. It is the barrier of not serving the poor: "for I was hungry and you gave me no food, I was thirsty and you gave me nothing to drink, I was a stranger and you did not welcome me, naked and you did not give me clothing, sick and in prison and you did not visit me" (Matt 25:42-43). The barrier to eternal life, in this famous story, is our own moral failing, our adherence to social and religious norms that exclude and set us apart from the "poor" who we fail to see as Christ.

In regard to physical deprivation, Jesus teaches clearly that neighbors reach out to those who need food, water, shelter, clothing—these most basic of human needs must be met in order for persons to attend to their full calling. In regard to social deprivation, Jesus teaches that no social barrier—ethnicity, race, gender, disease, mental illness, religious belief—can stand in the way of our reaching out to the neighbor. And none of these factors can serve as a means of putting a person or group beneath us, to use others as a means to an end, to own or subjugate them as property. In fact, what Jesus says to his disciples in the story of his anointing with the rich ointment is often omitted. In Mark's version we hear this line, "For you always have the poor with you, and you can show kindness to them whenever you wish; but you will not always have me" (Mark 14:7). Of course he has to explain to the disciples that the woman's anointing is for his burial (odd in itself since he is not yet dead), but they should not miss the sign that anointing is related to kingship, and he is about to be prosecuted for claiming to be "king of the Jews." But we rarely hear the middle phrase, perhaps because it was omitted by Matthew and John: "you can show kindness to them whenever you wish." Jesus seems to be saying that societies will always create categories of poor people. The call to discipleship is to recognize the ways in which people are subjected to impoverishment in all kinds of ways, but that disciples must cultivate a desire to overcome false categorizations and serve the poor out of love.

What today is called "social ministry" encompasses a full range of activities: social services for basic human needs such as food, shelter, and clothing; health-care ministries for the sick; prison ministries; orphanages and services for children; justice ministries that address systematic legal and economic issues; relief agencies—all of which operate on local, national, and international levels. The list goes on and on.

Again, it is important to distinguish the obligations of the Christian disciple to serve the poor and leading ministries of social mercy and justice on the part of the minister. Leading social ministries means galvanizing the community to service and providing the necessary means—educational, organizational, and financial—to help the church serve its mission to the poor, no matter who they are or what their condition. The charisms for leading ministries of mercy and justice are the virtue of seeing Christ in each person, knowledge about Christian social teachings and understanding about the contexts and people served, and the capacity to organize and mobilize resources for outreach, service, and systematic change.

The first charism is the gift of seeing Christ in every person and helping others to see Christ in every person. This is the gift of sight and recognition, which is of course related to empathy and compassion, especially for those who are society's outcast, lowly, poor, and rejected. Many of us can look around and fail to see those in our midst who are in need; in fact, it might be easier to label those who are poor as existing in some urban center or foreign country but not in our neighborhood. We cannot be moved by empathy and compassion if we are blind to

seeing those in our midst who are weeping. In Luke's story of the forgiven woman, Jesus turns to his dinner host and says, "Do you see this
woman? I entered your house; you gave me no water for my feet, but
she has bathed my feet with her tears and dried them with her hair"
(Luke 7:44). The minister is one gifted with seeing rightly, seeing their
neighbors suffering and poverty, and beginning to imagine ways of
liberating, healing, and restoring people's lives.

The gift of meeting Christ in every person is the capacity to recognize
each person's human dignity and to respond to them as one made in the
image of God. Ministries of social concern are rooted in the tradition of
both mercy and justice. Mercy, like compassion, is the tenderhearted
feeling one person has toward another, but especially in circumstances
where one has power over another. We think of appeals to judges,
political leaders, or victors of war to be merciful and not exact too hard
a sentence or punishment on the wrongdoer. It is also a way of speaking
about God's merciful love in relationship to the poor or the sinner. The
corporeal works of mercy in the Catholic tradition, based on Matthew 25
(visiting prisoners, providing shelter to the homeless, feeding the hungry,
giving drink to the thirsty, burying the dead, visiting the sick, and clothing the naked), point to the demand on those who have, those who have
power, and those who are able, to feel merciful to those suffering some
want.[25] Again, the works of mercy are the responsibility of all disciples;
ministers are called upon to lead disciples in service to the needy.

A capable minister of mercy and justice has received the gifts of compassion, empathy, and sympathy for the poor. They can understand their
own poverty and utter dependence on God and need for God's mercy.
And through this poverty they have received the prophet's vision to see
corruption and evil corroding human life and creation. The minister sees
the conditions for bigotry, hatred, racism, sexism, and economic oppression, but they also can see the possibilities for transforming social structures toward human well-being and flourishing. The practice of Christian
justice is not merely to meet the demands of fairness by the law but the
demands of neighbor relations. As Yahweh is just and righteous in upholding the covenant, the Israelites are called upon to be just to their
neighbor, especially the widow, orphan, and the poor. These are people
who find special favor with Yahweh because they are easily forgotten
by their neighbors. Justice is to live in right relationship to one another,

---

[25] The spiritual works of mercy are to instruct the ignorant, counsel the doubtful,
admonish sinners, bear wrongs patiently, forgive offenses willingly, comfort the
afflicted, pray for the living and the dead.

to nature, and to the creation. Mercy fuels justice to be righteous in mercy and love.

The second charism, related to knowing, is the gift of knowledge about the Christian tradition's teachings on mercy and social justice. In the Catholic tradition, over the past two centuries, the social teachings have developed around ten themes in a modern context: human dignity, the common good, preferential option for the poor, human rights, the principle of subsidiarity, economic justice, stewardship of creation, peace and disarmament, right to participation, and global solidarity and development. In addition to understanding justice in relationship to a broad range of social issues, ministers must also develop an understanding of the people and their social contexts, the causes of suffering, affliction, and oppression as they are manifest in particular settings.

A third charism is the gift for organizing resources in response to human needs and advocating for just systems. This is the gift of putting prophecy into action—the gifts for responding, creating systems and structures in which people are served, and animating the community with the call to mercy and justice. Practicing ministries of mercy and justice requires inviting the community to come to know the poor and marginalized in their midst, to experience compassion, solidarity and mercy for their situation, and to reflect on the gospel's demands for service. In addition, the ministry requires people who can organize the community's response, establish the necessary systems and structures to respond to the need, and empower disciples to carry forth this service.

Because of their complexity and prophetic demand, leading social ministries requires effective work in each of the practices of ministry—effective catechesis about the situation and the theological tradition, worship and preaching aimed at the conversion of our hearts toward the poor, pastoral care to address feelings of fear, loss, and the meaning of suffering, and administration for the wise use of the community's resources to serve the neighbor.

The Ministry of Leadership and Administration

Jesus lays the groundwork for compassionate and just leadership and administration of the community's resources to serve its mission. Clearly Jesus did not administer an organization or serve as a president or chief financial officer of a large enterprise. Organizationally, his group of followers is small and seemingly unorganized. And yet, out of this small group of followers, the church is born and a community settles in various places and develops organizational processes to steward its resources for its mission. The leadership of the community and oversight of its material goods and resources is essential to the community's presence and vitality in a local place. Without leadership and administration the church's mission would not have flourished. We can look to Jesus for two sources of leadership and administration: first is his identification as a servant and his teachings on household arrangements, and second is his relationship to the earth and creation.

The center of Jesus' ministry was not the synagogue, or what we might think of as a church in terms of a separate building, but rather the household, which served as the local center of business, worship, and social life for extended families. It is primarily in this setting that Jesus teaches and preaches (e.g., instructs the disciples and tells them how they are to enter houses: Mark 7:17; 10:10; 9:28; Matt 17:19; 13:36; Mark 6:10; Luke 9:4; 10:7), heals the sick (e.g., healing Simon's mother-in-law in Mark 1:29, 32-24; Matt 8:16; Luke 4:40-41; healing the paralytic who is lowered through the ceiling: Mark 2:1-12; Matt 9:1-8; Luke 5:17-26; healing Jarius's daughter: Mark 5:21-43; Matt 9:18-26), and shares meals, as was the custom in villages and towns (e.g., dining with tax collectors and sinners: Mark 2:15-17; Matt 9:9-13; Luke 5:27-32). Even when we read that Jesus taught in the "synagogue," the reference is to the assembly of the people rather than a separate building. Jesus taught, preached, and healed, then, where people commonly gathered in the Near Ancient world—the home. Early Christians would continue this pattern until the community grew so large that they needed separate buildings in which to worship and gather.

Jesus' relationship to households and families is not without critique, however. In fact, Jesus prophetically challenges the common assumptions about household arrangements and lays the ground for how the Christian community ought to think about its relationships and organizational structures. Families of Jesus' time were multigenerational, led by a father who arranged marriages, provided for women and slaves, and oversaw the economic, religious, and political aspects of family life. Jesus breaks with traditional family expectations in terms of relationships between fathers and women, siblings, stewards, and slaves. First, he becomes an itinerant preacher rather than staying within his household to serve his father. In fact, he boldly proclaims that everyone must leave his family to follow after him (Mark 10:28-31). Discipleship calls for a radical reorientation of human relationships in which Jesus proclaims that he has come to "set a man against his father, and a daughter against her mother, and a daughter-in-law against her mother-in-law" (Matt 10:34-36; Luke

12:51-53), and he goes so far as to claim that disciples "hate" their family (Luke 14:26; Mark 10:37). The true family is the one that does God's will (Mark 3:31-35; Matt 12:46-50; Luke 8:19-21).

It is little wonder that people questioned his judgment, for Jesus was asking people to leave behind every possible form of security as well as identity and filial love. It would have been hard to believe that Jesus' small group of followers would receive a new family beyond anything they could imagine (Matt 19:29; Luke 18:30; Mark 10:30), but that is the radical nature of Jesus' call to discipleship. Jesus promises a new family, but as Ritva Williams points out, it is a family "based not on biological kinship relations" but on new mutual relationships under "one father" who is God (Matt 23:9).[26] Jesus may seem to be excluding human fathers from this new family, asking disciples to relate as brothers, sisters, and mothers, but he is claiming that new families will not be dominated by patriarchal forms of male leadership in which the father had control over the lives of the whole household. Jesus seems to be critiquing a distinctive form of household leadership that kept certain members bound by strict rules and laws.

Jesus is establishing a new kind of household arrangement and management, one based on radical inclusiveness of all people in relationship to one another. To demonstrate what he means he teaches the disciples that "whoever wishes to become great among you must be your servant, and whoever wishes to be first among you must be slave of all. For the Son of Man came not to be served but to serve, and to give his life a ransom for many" (Mark 10:43-44). Jesus evokes two contemporary images: the servant, one who was employed for service in a household, and a slave, one who was owned as property and was not free to choose employment (though they could be paid). To be a servant, Jesus is pointing to the kind of relationships of service that the community is bound by, and in turn the ways in which leadership in the community is to function in contrast to worldly leaders who "lord it over" people and are tyrants. In addition to the servant image, Jesus tells his disciples to be slaves, a teaching Jesus has been pushing through the entire Mark narrative. It means to give up any personal claim on oneself, to belong completely to Christ, to be "owned" by God's mission as it is being taken up by Christ, on the way to the cross. Jesus takes the position of a servant and slave when he washes the feet of his disciples and Paul refers to

---

[26] Ritva H. Williams, *Stewards, Prophets, Keepers of the Word* (Peabody, MA: Hendrickson Publishers Inc., 2006), 30.

Jesus' obedience as that of a slave (Phil 2:5-11). The images of Isaiah's Suffering Servant echo in the texts about Jesus' suffering and death.

Jesus does in fact assume the position of a servant and slave when he literally washes the feet of the disciples, as was the custom in households (John 13:1-15). But the meaning of being a servant shifts in Jesus' act: those who are to follow him are to imitate him, not only in washing each others' feet (John 13:14), but in loving each other as friends and laying down their lives for their friends (John 15:12-14). Jesus overcomes the dominant models of service as what one is required to do for another in the role of servant or slave. As Sandra Schneiders points out, friendship as the model of service overturns domination, superiority, and inferiority in social position. In washing their feet, Jesus models true love of friends.[27] Being a friend in John's case means following Jesus to the cross; being baptized means plunging into the death of Christ.

In addition to servants and slaves, Jesus speaks frequently about stewards, men who were either slaves or free, and who served as household managers, overseeing the finances, land, food, and material resources needed to sustain the family household. Depending on the size of the household and wealth of the family, stewards could have a great deal of power and influence. Not always held in high esteem, stewards were viewed as shrewd businessmen, expected to be loyal to their master and crafty in their dealings in order to secure what was necessary. They served as a type of broker for their master, a go-between, and a representative to traders and other businesspeople. A disloyal steward was one who sought personal financial gain and was disloyal toward their master. In Jesus' parables of the stewards, he is offering an example of discipleship and those who would be leaders in the community (Luke 12:41-48; 16:1-8). The good steward, in the absence of their master, is faithful, wise, and prudent. As Williams points out, Luke's view of a "leader in the *ekklesia* is to see him or herself as a steward, an agent for God and Christ." As a leader, a steward is diligent and even shrewd in "promoting and actualizing God's alternative vision of justice."[28]

Paul continues the model of the steward and slave as exemplary of community leadership. He calls himself a "slave" of Christ (Rom 1:1; Phil 1:1; Gal 1:10) and a "servant of Christ and steward [*oikonomous*] of God's mysteries" (Gal 4:1), comparing himself to one who is called to manage the master's household resources. Williams points out that when

---

[27] Sandra M. Schneiders, *Written That You May Believe: Encountering Jesus in the Fourth Gospel* (New York: Crossroad, 1999), 162–74.

[28] Williams, *Stewards, Prophets, Keepers*, 76.

Paul claims himself as Christ's steward he is claiming that he is both appointed by Christ and responsible and accountable to Christ (1 Cor 4:2-6); stewardship is the source of his authority and apostleship as well as his responsibility. Like Jesus, Paul reverses the social order, claiming to be a slave, a servant as a position of leadership, and calling to task anyone who attempts to claim a higher social status and forget their kinship to other members of the community (Gal 3:25-29). The model of steward recalls that what is "managed" is not one's own resources but gifts from God.

In later Pauline writings *oikonomous* is associated with *episkopos* (overseer or bishop), the one who oversees God's resources on behalf of the community because they have the capacity to oversee their own household (1 Tim 3:1-5). The image is a way to describe God's broker, a mediator, and one who is responsible for serving the needs of the community. As Williams points out, however, it is not long after the New Testament canon is formed that early patristic writers take up the images of patriarchal leadership over households as the form of Christian leadership, reversing forms of social status that Jesus sought to overcome.

Another important aspect of Jesus' life and ministry that is related to the sixth practice of ministry is his relationship to the earth. As noted in the first chapter, stewardship is about overseeing the household but it is also related to the responsibility to care for the whole creation. Jesus teaches about God as one who provides and protects creation, everything from the birds of the air to wildflowers (Matt 6:26). He boldly proclaims that we need not be overly preoccupied with food or clothing (Matt 6:25) since God provides everything we need through creation. In the parables, Jesus employs images from agriculture including seeds, vineyards, harvests, and animals such as sheep and fish. Jesus' profound sense of God's abundant presence and activity in the created world points to his sense of stewardship in treating all creation as a gift of God given for our well-being. Both the incarnation and the resurrection point to the claim that God enters into the world, is part of the world, and is redeeming the whole creation that "has been groaning in labor pains" to its completion (Rom 8:22).

Jesus' embodiment as servant, slave, and steward lays the foundation for the Christian community's practice of leading and administrating its organizational processes and structures. The three charisms are to understand the vision necessary for the community, managing and administering its resources, and the virtue of building up the body through identifying many charisms and vocations. Clearly all six practices of ministry comprise leadership in ministry, but based on contemporary writings on leadership, there are particular charisms for leadership that are important to identify. Since leadership is not defined today by a particular style, such as a charismatic personality, it is important to identify the capacities we look for when we seek good leadership.

The first charism is the gift of vision. Leaders are people who can articulate the community's vision out of its mission and garner the necessary resources to make that vision a reality. Despite the fact that scholars who study leadership cannot agree on a definition, they do agree that vision is one of the driving capacities of a leader. Lovett Weems argues that "leadership is about change," which requires a leader to take a community's mission and envision how and in what ways it can live out that mission in a particular concrete historical time and place. Change, in the sense of renewal, regeneration, and strategic thinking, is necessary for an organization to adapt and respond to situations in order to thrive and not grow stagnant.

The gift of vision means the Spirit blesses persons with the knowledge of foresight: the ability to see ahead; to discern barriers, problems, and consequences to various options and choices; and to envision a way forward in the concrete and particular circumstances the community faces. Such vision is a knowledge that is both broad and particular. A leader with vision does not gain this sight alone, however, but rather the gift includes the capacity to discern with the people where and how to move forward, to articulate, even when it is not always clear, how the community should live out its mission in the present and near future. As Weems points out, vision is not the same as mission: the mission is "what we exist to do" and the vision is "what God is calling us to do in the immediate future."[29] In this regard he claims that organizational vision is unique to each group, whereas the mission of similar institutions may be quite similar. Congregations, for example, exist to gather believers into communion for the sake of the gospel's mission. The vision for each congregation is unique because the setting, situation, location, and people in each congregation are particular. Vision points to the future, according to Weems, but it is realistic and grounded in reality. It fosters hope and yet demands change; and sometimes facing change is a painful and fearful process for people. Visions invite people to imagine the new.

The second charism of leadership is the gifts to manage and administer. Excellent leadership requires both knowing and understanding the

[29] Lovett H. Weems Jr., *Church Leadership: Vision, Team, Culture and Integrity* (Nashville, TN: Abingdon Press, 1993), 42.

mission and vision and the capacity to mobilize that into action. It is too often the case that management and administration are not considered to be ministries but just a necessary part of work. Nevertheless, every minister is involved at some level in managing and administering the community's resources, and leaders of church organizations such as congregations, schools, colleges and universities, and hospitals, are immersed in the day-to-day reality of administering and managing large and complex systems. Perhaps we hold on to a similar view of stewards from the first century. There is something clearly "worldly" about the realities of finance, legal and computer systems, buildings, and investments, which cannot be counted as holy work in the way that worship is viewed. But if we separate the work of administering and managing from the rest of ministry, we miss a crucial dimension of the call and practice. It is necessary to recall the teaching of Saint Benedict: "The cellarer must regard all utensils and goods of the monastery as sacred vessels of the altar, aware that nothing is to be neglected" (RB 31). Administration and management is the gift to recognize that all the material goods of the organization are gifts from God and part of God's creation, which require wise and prudent stewardship.

Lovett Weems defines administration as "doing things right" and management as "doing the right things." Administering an organization or program includes following the policies and procedures of the organization that allow people to work together toward its goals and mission. Management has to do with understanding what structures, policies, and processes are needed to sustain and carry forward the work. One of the important charisms for ministers is the gift of knowing what organizational systems are needed, how they work, and what needs to happen within an organization to ensure that the mission and vision are served (e.g., finance, personnel, physical plant, strategic planning, and systems management).

The charism of being is the capacity to see gifts in others and to mobilize the charisms and vocations within the community for building up the body. It is the gift commonly referred to today as team building. No effective leader can work alone; they must lead others in carrying out the vision and mission of the organization. This requires building community, a sense of shared purpose, effective communication and governance practices, shared decision making, and transparency. The bigger the organization, the larger the task, but building an effective team of people to work together has many of the same features. According to Weems it involves recognizing who are key leaders and stakeholders in an organization, empowering them to carry out their work, and helping them to contribute to the work of the whole. Team building requires the moral capacities to respect each person and his or her point of view; knowing how to involve people and foster the flourishing of their gifts; creating effective collaboration and sharing power; communicating effectively and clearly; and recognizing, developing, and honoring people and their contributions. A leader's charism for team building requires that they not be afraid or threatened by others' gifts, but rather that they see it as their vocation to identify the charisms and vocations of people in the community and foster them for the good of the community.

This chapter has been an all-too-brief overview of Jesus' ministry and the Spirit's charisms for the six practices of ministry. Clearly much more can be said about each practice and charism. By drawing out some of the main features of Jesus' ministry and identifying some of the central charisms that form the basis of the practices of ministry, we can begin to see how God's two hands give birth to the church's ministry in all times and places. The ministries of leading the community by teaching, preaching, leading worship and prayer, pastoral care, social ministry, and administration have endured throughout the Christian tradition in various forms and styles, but they have endured precisely because of their Christological and pneumatological foundations. We turn now to a discussion of what constitutes a practice.

Sources for Further Reading

Clebsch, William A., and Charles R. Jaekle. *Pastoral Care in Historical Perspective.* New York: Harper Torchbooks, 1967.

Fiorenza, Elisabeth Schüssler. *In Memory of Her: A Feminist Theological Reconstruction of Christian Origins.* New York: Crossroad, 1983.

Gerkin, Charles V. *An Introduction to Pastoral Care.* Nashville, TN: Abingdon Press, 1997.

Groome, Thomas H. *Sharing Faith: A Comprehensive Approach to Religious Education and Pastoral Ministry.* San Francisco, CA: HarperCollins, 1991.

Haight, Roger. *Dynamics of Theology.* Mahwah, NJ: Paulist Press, 1990.

Herzog, William R., II. *Prophet and Teacher: An Introduction to the Historical Jesus.* Louisville, KY: Westminster John Knox Press, 2005.

Hovda, Robert W. *Strong, Loving and Wise: Presiding in Liturgy*. Collegeville, MN: Liturgical Press, 1983.

Karris, Robert. *Luke: Artist and Theologian*. New York: Paulist Press, 1985.

Kavanagh, Aidan. *Elements of Rite: A Handbook of Liturgical Style*. New York: Pueblo Publishing Co., 1982.

Korgen, Jeffry Odell. *My Lord and My God: Engaging Catholics in Social Ministry*. Mahwah, NJ: Paulist Press, 2007.

Long, Thomas G. *The Witness of Preaching*. Louisville, KY: Westminster/John Knox Press, 1989.

McCurley, Foster R. *Social Ministry in the Lutheran Tradition*. Minneapolis, MN: Fortress Press, 2008.

O'Collins, Gerald. *Jesus: A Portrait*. Maryknoll, NY: Orbis Books, 2008.

Osmer, Richard Robert. *A Teachable Spirit: Recovering the Teaching Office in the Church*. Louisville, KY: Westminster/John Knox Press, 1990.

Palmer, Parker K. *To Know as We Are Known: A Spirituality of Education*. San Francisco, CA: Harper & Row, 1983.

Patton, John. *Pastoral Care: An Essential Guide*. Nashville, TN: Abingdon Press, 2005.

Remus, Harold. *Jesus as Healer*. New York: Cambridge University Press, 1997.

Saliers, Don E. *Worship as Theology: Foretaste of Glory Divine*. Nashville, TN: Abingdon Press, 1994.

Schneiders, Sandra M. *Written That You May Believe: Encountering Jesus in the Fourth Gospel*. New York: Crossroad, 1999.

Stairs, Jean. *Listening for the Soul: Pastoral Care and Spiritual Direction*. Minneapolis, MN: Fortress Press, 2000.

Stevenson-Moessner, Jeanne. *A Primer in Pastoral Care*. Minneapolis: Fortress Press, 2005.

Ulrich, Tom. *Parish Social Ministry*. Notre Dame, IN: Ave Marie Press, 2001.

Veling, Terry. *Practical Theology: "On Earth as It Is in Heaven."* Maryknoll, NY: Orbis Books, 2005.

Weems, Lovett H., Jr. *Church Leadership: Vision, Team, Culture and Integrity*. Nashville, TN: Abingdon Press, 1993.

White, James F. *Introduction to Christian Worship*. 3rd rev. ed. Nashville, TN: Abingdon Press, 2000.

Williams, Ritva H. *Stewards, Prophets, Keepers of the Word*. Peabody, MA: Hendrickson Publishers Inc., 2006.

Chapter 5

Chapter 5

Understanding Ministry as Practice

Throughout the previous chapters, I have been describing ministry as a practice, and in this chapter I want to offer a detailed description of what is considered a practice. The concept of practice and practices has recently gained widespread attention among philosophers, social scientists, and theologians, and several of these ideas prove helpful in describing ministry as a practice. First, a practice is understood as an intentional action, which, secondly, takes place within a community and tradition of shared meaning and purpose. Third, practice is an embodied action, an expression of identity, knowledge, and conviction through bodily action. Fourth, practices are corruptible, meaning they are intertwined in personal sin and failings as well as oppressive forms of systematic power and evil. And fifth, practice is a spiritual exercise that requires attention to the immanent and transcendent presence of God.

Defining Practice

I have defined ministry as encompassing six basic practices, each of which, taken on its own, can be described as discrete actions. For example, to provide pastoral care to the sick requires that a minister speak and listen, pray and counsel, interpret and guide. When preparing to preach, the pastor must read and study, write and rehearse, and deliver the sermon and listen for response. Each of these acts corresponds to the dictionary definition of an action: "the bringing about of an alteration"; an action is the "manner or method of performing" as well as "an act of will."[1] An action is "a thing done, a deed." An action, then, involves deliberation of choices, selection, and the execution of that choice, the doing of something, in order to alter or bring about a change in a condition.

We perform actions all day long—washing our face, making coffee, driving a car, and skydiving—some that are repeated and others performed only once in a lifetime. Practices are made up of actions, but this does not mean that all actions are practices. The term "practices" commonly refers to actions that are repeated over time with intention in a patterned way. The dictionary defines "practice" as "to do or perform often, customarily, or habitually"; "to perform or work at repeatedly so as to become proficient"; and "to train by repeated exercises."[2] In understanding practice, action is an essential component. As James Nieman points out, practices are not the same as an action but are more properly understood as a "group of component actions that have been shaped into a larger pattern."[3]

The medieval theologian Thomas Aquinas was interested in human action as a moral reality that involves choice, intention, and knowledge.[4] An action that is moral is not involuntary behavior, but rather is an action that an agent is responsible for, and we can praise or blame a person for what they have done. Aquinas distinguishes two aspects of an action, both of which can be judged good or bad: the way it is done and the reason for doing it. An action may be done well but have immoral intentions, as in the case of the good thief. The good thief acquires an excellent skill that can be praised: they steal well. But, in Aquinas' view, an action is more than technique: the moral quality has to do with the end or the good toward which the action aims. Most of us would agree that the thief's aim in stealing another person's belongings is not morally good, so the act is not a good moral action. An important element, then, in appraising human actions is the question, "Why is this being done?" We can inquire about the purpose of an act, the end it hopes to achieve, and

---

[1] *Merriam-Webster's Collegiate Dictionary*, 11th ed., s.v. "action."

[2] Ibid., s.v. "practice."

[3] James Nieman, "Why the Idea of Practice Matters," in *Teaching Preaching as a Christian Practice*, eds. Thomas G. Long and Leonora Tubbs Tisdale (Louisville, KY: Westminster John Knox Press, 2008), 21.

[4] Saint Thomas Aquinas, *Summa Theologica*, trans. Fathers of the English Dominican Province (New York: Benziger Brothers Inc., 1947), I–II, qq. 6–20.

this, for Aquinas, is how we understand and classify acts as moral and immoral—by the ends toward which they aim.

Aquinas identified two important features of an action that are essential to understanding how a "group of component actions" make up a practice—the "why" or intent of the practice and the "how" or the way it is carried out. Undoubtedly, Aquinas was concerned with the moral intent and not as nearly interested in the how, or the way something is done. In applying his theory of action to the practice of ministry, a minister must desire and know the good toward which they intend their acts. In this sense the practices of ministry aim toward serving God and disciples in ways that help discipleship to flourish for God's mission in the world. In Aquinas' anthropology, both the mind and the will are involved: we desire the good, we know the end we seek, we deliberate about the best way to achieve the end, we choose the means, and execute the act. In this regard, the practice of ministry is deemed ministry (for not everything a minister does is ministry) when it is understood and recognized by others as an intentional act aimed at a recognizable and commonly accepted good—in this case the building up of the community for the sake of discipleship. A minister should be able to respond to the question, "Why do you do that?" The aim of a ministry act should be consciously known and chosen.

But in today's thinking about practice, the how, or the agency to carry forth the practices of ministry, is deemed vitally important. Both aspects, we will see, are part of a more comprehensive view of the components of a practice. Practices of ministry can be deemed good or bad in terms of the technique, skill, and performance of the action as well as the intent. In this regard, the "how" of practices point to capacities and levels of competence. For instance, a local church decides to host a program to welcome back parishioners who are not active or have left the church. Their proximate aim is to provide an opportunity for people to consider becoming active members, to reengage their faith within the church community, and to be "full, active and conscious" disciples. Such an intention is certainly morally good, but we would be suspect of the program if the ministers also, or only, intended to increase membership in order to raise more money or to demonstrate to other churches that they are the biggest and the best in town. Intention clearly matters.

The pastor and committee could, however, have good intentions but execute the meeting poorly. In this case, the goal or the aim is not achieved—good intention alone does not bring about good practice. We would deem the pastor, or the committee, incompetent if they conducted the ministry poorly. Generally, both incompetence in practice and immoral intentions disappoint and make people angry, though we tend to be more forgiving and tolerant of incompetence, at least when we judge the person's intentions to be good. Nevertheless, incompetence in ministry over a long period of time also leads to waning discipleship—people will look elsewhere for leadership.

Christian Practices in Community

Practices are not individual acts carried out by a single person; rather they are social and communal patterned actions. As Nieman notes, practices are "common" insofar as they are produced by groups in order to serve their interests. Practices have "common origins and goals" that emerge from "long-standing patterns and ways of being" that "serve collective outcomes, creating mutual goods."[5] This view of practices highlights the person as a social being and as an inheritor of social practices. Practitioners are part of a community, which bears the intent, meaning, and know-how of the practice.

In one sense, practices are the things ordinary people do in their lives that constitute patterns, traditions, and customs in shared communal life. Practices are a basic human reality that can be found around the world, infused with the meaning, value, and purpose of their religious and cultural contexts. In other words, practices are an anthropological constant, but there is no such thing as generic practices. The meaning and values embedded within practices is a contextual and historical reality. For example, practices of witness are widespread, yet take on different meanings and patterns in different cultural contexts. We think of the difference between preachers such as John the Baptist, Francis of Assisi, and Martin Luther King Jr., each who gained a widespread public following because of their speech and message, but who did so within very definite traditions of public witness.

In their theological writings on Christian practices, Dorothy Bass and Craig Dykstra emphasize that Christian practices are human practices that have theological and normative content because they are interpreted through the gospel. "Christian practices are patterns of cooperative human activity in and through which life together takes shape over time

---

[5] Nieman, "Why the Idea of Practice Matters," 22.

in response to and in the light of God as known in Jesus Christ."[6] Christian practices contain claims about both what God is doing in the world and what our response to God entails. Practices "resist the separation of thinking from acting," of Christian teaching from the life of faith. Practices are not just "doing" something, but a "group of component actions" that expresses a set of fundamental convictions and beliefs about who we are as Christians, what we claim about God, and our life as God's creation. Beliefs and ideas about God do not exist separately from life and action, but are constitutive of practices, so that both the way we do something and the intention express a theological and faith reality. Take, for example, table fellowship. I noted earlier that Jesus broke the social norms that defined who was acceptable to eat with and who was not. Not long ago in the United States, African American citizens could not eat in certain restaurants or take a drink from a water fountain. More powerful perhaps than any words spoken by the white community, these table fellowship practices defined the boundaries of who is acceptable and who is not. Table fellowship practices are not generic either, but deeply embedded in cultural and social contexts in which the patterned action carries meaning, beliefs, and interpretation within that community.

In this sense, practices are what make up the life of discipleship. In fact we could say that the seven features of discipleship, described in the first chapter, are basic human practices that through baptism make us into Christian "practitioners." We can see that the seven features are in fact human practices embraced worldwide: following a teacher, worshiping in community, witnessing to the truth, reaching out to neighbors, offering forgiveness, fighting injustices, and stewarding the resources of the earth and the community. I described these practices as Christian practices of Christian discipleship because of their meaning in light of the life, death, and resurrection of Christ. Christians, over time, have interpreted human practices through a wide variety of beliefs, symbols, and stories. Consider the example of the practice of hospitality: communities in all times and places have formed practices related to welcoming guests or strangers in their midst, and Christians have interpreted this human practice as a Christian practice when it bears certain intention, purpose, and know-how. Key biblical stories mark the Christian

---

[6] Craig Dykstra and Dorothy C. Bass, "A Theological Understanding of Christian Practices," in *Practicing Theology: Beliefs and Practices in Christian Life*, eds. Miroslav Volf and Dorothy C. Bass (Grand Rapids, MI: Wm. B. Eerdmans, 2002), 3.

practice of hospitality: Abraham welcomes three strangers, Jesus washes the feet of his disciples, Saint Benedict emphasizes that the monastery must welcome every guest as Christ, and a local food pantry sponsored by three area churches turns no one away. The practice—both the doing and its intention—have a theological and normative claim: as Christians we treat a guest this way in our community because we believe the guest is a person created by God, bearing the *imago Dei*, and in them we see Christ himself. As Bass and Dykstra state, practices are "things Christian people do together over time to address fundamental human needs in response to and in the light of God's active presence for the life of the world."[7]

Communal and Tradition-Based Practices

What distinguishes most contemporary definitions of practice from Aquinas's or the dictionary is the emphasis on understanding practices in terms of social and historical contexts. Practices are shared actions, performed over time, that carry meaning and purpose in communities; they are not isolated, individual acts. Sabbath-keeping practices are not something we make up and do on our own; rather we participate in a community that shares belief in the meaning and purpose as well as the duties to be carried forth on the Sabbath. Even if we each design our own Sabbath practices, the very notion of Sabbath comes from a long tradition of Jewish and Christian story, symbol, and ritual.

Terrence Tilley has developed a practical theology of tradition that defines tradition as "a set of enduring practices" or a "set of linked practices."[8] It is common, particularly in the study of theology, to consider tradition in terms of the development of doctrine: the way in which fundamental beliefs and teachings, such as Christology or the Trinity, developed in the context of differing philosophical and theological movements. But, according to Tilley, tradition is not composed of ideas that

[7] Ibid., 18. Dorothy C. Bass's work focuses on twelve practices: keeping Sabbath, honoring the body, hospitality, household economics, saying yes and saying no, testimony, discernment, shaping communities, forgiveness, healing, dying well, and singing. See the web site for a complete list of the project's publications: http://www.practicingourfaith.org/.

[8] Terrence W. Tilley, *Inventing Catholic Tradition* (Maryknoll, NY: Orbis Books, 2001), 57.

are handed on from one generation to the next; rather the act of passing on the practices of the faith, received and formed within particular cultural contexts, constitutes what we mean by a "living tradition." "Traditions serve to confer identity on a community of people . . . provide a sense of stability, a communal space in which people can dwell, and a set of practices that shape how the participants live in the world."[9]

Tradition, as a "set of enduring practices," is formed in two ways. Practices are "given" to us, passed down from previous generations, and "practiced" by people who influence our actions and thoughts. Anyone who has "received" a tradition knows how strong the "given" quality of traditions can appear. This is certainly true of family customs, such as the giving of certain Christmas gifts and meal practices, or the liturgical practice of bowing in the presence of the Eucharist, or call-and-response patterns of African American preaching. Tilley notes how traditions are "*perceived* as stable, continuous, and certain."[10] Oftentimes because of their strength and stability they are experienced as unchanging, static, and immobile, which is captured in the line every community offers for its reason for not changing a practice: "it's always been done this way."

And yet, people are agents of traditions: they make traditions through receiving and adapting practices in everyday contexts. At times this is a conscious and deliberate choice, particularly when traditions are in flux or practices are called into question, and at other times pressures outside a community, such as disease, war, or economic influences can cause a shift in practices. Rarely do practices change because one person decides to do something differently. Because practices are social and communal it takes time for new actions and meanings to be grafted onto a practice, but as Tilley points out "traditions mutate, sometimes radically, as they are passed on."[11]

This is all to say that tradition lives primarily in the concrete daily practices that people embody together, and constitutive of those practices are the beliefs, values, and intentions that both give meaning and rationale to practices: we do this because we believe this and we believe this and so we do this. The act and its intention are intertwined. The connective tissue of practices is what Tilley calls the "grammar" of the practice: those "inferred rules that show how means (material means and skills) and ends are connected in the patterns of actions that constitute the

---

[9] Ibid., 43.
[10] Ibid.
[11] Ibid., 30.

practice."[12] By rules of a practice, Tilley means both the written and unwritten codes that communities follow, so that we learn the grammar of a practice by engaging in it over time. We learn the practices of Christian discipleship by being immersed in a community of practice. We learn to practice hospitality, prayer, and forgiveness, and only later reflect on the ways in which the community carries out this particular practice, with this intent, and according to a particular grammar. Reflection on practice comes along well after practices are encoded into our lives; it can come as a refreshing insight into the deeper meaning of a practice, particularly when we encounter practices different from our own, or when practices embody corrupt and immoral views that demand to be critiqued and changed.

In the tradition of Christian practice and belief, ministers are vitally important carriers and creators of tradition because they are interpreters of practice, both in the meaning practices embody and the way they are expressed. Ministers are authorities of practice within a tradition in at least three ways.

First, ministers learn the practices of discipleship and ministry that have endured in the Christian tradition from its inception. These practices are not rigid, static, or immutable but have been adapted and are changing over time as they are practiced within particular communities of faith. Ministers receive a community's understanding of these practices and what their role and responsibility is as teacher, administrator, social justice minister, and so on. There is a received and accepted body of actions and patterns within each practice that ministers come to know by growing up in a community of faith. The acceptable actions and patterns of each practice also bear a tradition of knowledge, belief, meaning, and purpose. When students learn the practice of ministry they begin to read and understand the assumptions about the practices of their community that they may have taken for granted. In undergoing formation in acquiring skill for a practice and in understanding its purpose and meaning, ministers early in their career usually have a heightened sense of what they are doing and why. Education should heighten a sense of the "grammar" of practice, what holds together the act and the intention. Practices of ministry, then, are both inherited and learned.

---

[12] Ibid., 54. For more on rules and practice, see Tilley, "The Grammar of Tradition," 88–122.

Second, a minister becomes a minister in and through the practice of ministry. They receive a tradition of practice, they study the meaning of the practice, but it is neither in repeating what others have done nor memorizing theories of practice that they "become" a minister. It is in the practice, combined with knowledge of the received tradition and contemporary insights and critiques, repeated over time in which the person and the practice become integrated in one life and vocation. (I will examine this claim more fully in the next chapter.)

Third, ministers are, in Tilley's terms, agents of tradition as a creative and constructive process in time and history. They are not the sole agents of tradition, to be sure, but ministers play a vital role in tending the practices of the community and providing interpretation and meaning of practices within a tradition. They do inherit practices from the past, but their role is not to force the community into a set of practices as practiced in the past but rather to embody and understand the purposes (the meanings and values) of received practices within a contemporary context.

Ministers stand in an interesting place within a tradition. In situations where the community has forgotten the meaning of a practice, they can *retrieve* a practice and give it new purpose. In situations in which a practice has become so solidified that the community cannot change, a minister can be a catalyst for a *change* in practice. In times when the culture has moved against the received practice and its wisdom, ministers must encourage the community to remain *faithful* to its tradition. In times when the community rejects its practices, the minister must be *prophetic* and challenge people to grasp the wisdom embedded in its practices. Leading the practices of discipleship, then, requires a great deal of wisdom about the received tradition that the minister is responsible to pass on, and the contemporary conditions in which disciples search to live out these practices in a meaningful way. The practice of ministry is first and foremost attention to the practices of discipleship in community.

Embodied Practice

In terms of action and practice the body is not inconsequential. In fact, it is central, although Aquinas and the system of theology built on his thought did not pay much attention to embodied practice. Aquinas was keen to figure out the human process prior to external bodily movement, in other words how the mind and the will, or the intellect and desire, work in consort to know and choose what is good. Today we would understand this internal bodily process of the brain and mind as a bodily act. This is a complex activity in itself, since the mind must search for all the possible means to achieve the end, including the various consequences that attend each choice. Aquinas called this mental process "counsel," by which he means a process of discernment that examines choices and reaches a conclusion about the best way to proceed. Once the will chooses, the mind commands the person to act. As noted before, he was less interested in what happens when an action is actually carried out; everything interesting for him is prior to such engagement.

But actions and practices are not only mental but also physical and bodily acts. The five senses have long been understood as the primary entry of human experience and knowledge: we come to know the world through our experience of sight, sound, touch, taste, and smell. These are primary bodily information systems. Not only do we take in information through the five senses, but we process that information, interpret it, and react to it. Our reactions are not referred to as senses, but as expressive acts that involve emotions, thoughts, and physicality: we speak, gesture, make a facial expression, adopt a stance or posture, and do something. Actions are dialogical in a sense; they are reactions to information from the environment through the body and a sending out of information through the body to the environment. The embodied person is a living conversation, or self-in-dialogue, as a self-reflexive agent; at the same time this self-in-dialogue is acting, responding, and engaging in action with others and their contexts. It is this point of practice that is most difficult to get at, since it is doing something that is interactive, performative, and expressive of the self-in-relationship all at once.

Practices require bodies. Practices are not concepts in our minds but rather enacted and inscribed actions that take place in relationship in the world. They express who we are and what we intend, usually. The body has become a central focus of Christian theology and spirituality in recent years, fueled by the attempt to rid ourselves of the long-standing dualisms of flesh and spirit, body and soul, which often degraded the body in negative terms or dismissed it as a site of religious experience and knowledge. But Christian theology has retrieved a more positive view of the body based on its claims of creation (Gen 1), the incarnation of God entering bodily existence (John 1:14), the resurrection of the body (1 Cor 15), and the church as the Body of Christ (1 Cor 10:16).

In addition to the Christological significance of the body, there is also a pneumatological dimension to the body. Paul points out, after a long discussion of the sin of fornication, that bodies are united to God through the Spirit and therefore are to express in what they do that the body is a holy dwelling place: "Or do you not know that your body is a temple of the Holy Spirit within you, which you have from God, and that you are not your own? For you were bought with a price; therefore glorify God in your body" (1 Cor 6:19-20). In other words, we are what we act. As the new temple, the body of the disciple becomes the site for expressing the practices that constitute the way of life of discipleship. Charisms, gifts of the Spirit, are an embodied gift, received within the body and expressed in and through the body in each person's vocation.

The practice of ministry is an embodied practice in at least two regards. First, is the realization that leading disciples in the way of discipleship is about taking up a set of embodied practices. For example, Stephanie Paulsell, in *Honoring the Body: Meditations on a Christian Practice*, describes how Christians have interpreted and embraced various practices of caring for the body because of our claims about the God of creation, incarnation, sacrament, and redemption. She demonstrates how ordinary human practices of the body become religious practices inscribed with particular theological meaning. Our ritual acts are deeply rooted in common practices of caring for the body: we cleanse and ritually bathe the body in the waters of baptism, we feed and nourish our bodies with food and drink at the eucharistic table, we engage Sabbath practices to rest from our labor, and we anoint sick bodies and soothe their suffering. These practices are largely inherited from the tradition and enacted in particular ways in communities, but they are also places where disciples can express, imagine, and re-create the faith through enacting practices in new ways. The practices of discipleship require intentional and embodied action and ministers help to guide this practice through critical appropriation, not sheer repetition, of communal and tradition-based practices within the contemporary context of the community. Intentional practice requires discernment by the community: how do we, for example, embody honor of the body in a faithful way in our time and place?

Second, ministry is an embodied practice. If vocation is rooted in charisms and the body is the temple of the Spirit, the charisms for the practices of ministry are embodied expressions of the Spirit's gifts. As with any practice, it is not difficult to see that ministry requires a body to act, react, and enact: mouths that speak, ears that listen, eyes that see, hands that touch, a spine that bears weight and holds posture, lungs that breathe, brains that think, and faces that communicate. The body is necessary to carry forth the six practices, but not as a mechanical function. How the minister practices in and through the body becomes an expression of who the minister is and what they intend. In practice, action is embodied incarnated communication.

We are often quite unconscious of our bodies in practice until we have to learn something new. Bodies have to learn to wash dishes, brush teeth, and thread a needle. Learning to play a musical instrument requires practicing scales, learning fingering on an instrument, and reading music. Likewise, preaching the word of God in the assembly is not automatic even for the most gifted public speaker. It is an embodied practice that is learned over time. Most ministry students learning to preach become very conscious of their bodies: they may feel embarrassed about how they look, their throat is dry, they feel shy and blush, struggle to make eye contact with the listeners, and do not project their voice well. The body requires training in how to preach in order to become a good, even excellent, preacher: the practice of the body must be intentional over time for the enactment of the preaching and the message to become one.

The same is true for all the practices of ministry. The initial learning stages are filled with bodily awareness: the chaplain feels fear in the pit of his stomach as he approaches the room of a terminally ill patient; the presider does not know how high to lift her hands; the administrator leads a meeting, forgetting to offer a break; the social justice minister's legs ache from standing in a soup kitchen line; the catechist is unaware of how long she has been speaking to a class. The body in some cases is giving information in terms of feelings and discomfort, but the body can also be ignored and forgotten. Good practice over time attends to the body, what it is telling us, but also remembers the body as integral to the practice undertaken.

The Corruptibility of Practice

Practices are not neutral, nor are they always good. The meanings, values, and beliefs we hold most dear are embedded deeply within practices, sometimes known to us, and sometimes hidden. Practices can have a range of corrupting influences from the problem of forgetfulness or inattention, to selfish motives, to power and domination that are wrapped insidiously in and through basic daily practices. Each of these kinds of corruptibility is present in any Christian practice, including the practices of ministry. In other words, there is no pure practice, no perfectly rendered practice of pure intent and embodiment. Practices, as embodied actions of human persons-in-community, reflect the very human-ness of the actors and their communities.

The first type of corruptibility in a practice happens through sheer repetition of the act over time. The sheer force of habit obscures the meaning, intention, and purpose of a practice. The practice continues, perhaps with vague or general intention, but the intention gets buried so deep in the action that it becomes forgotten or lost. It does not animate the practice, or the person, in a powerful way. The old saying, "we have always done it this way," is an apt illustration of the act continuing yet severed from its purpose.

For example, a person can attend Sunday worship services but how is this practice honoring the Sabbath? They may attend church each week but not be fully aware of why they are there or what is happening. Jack goes to church each Sunday because he believes that God has commanded it and the church requires it, but he does not pay attention or fully participate in the responses or singing. The practice has become so routinized and habitual that neither the doing of the act or its intention is clearly known and embraced by Jack. Jack may have a good intention regarding Sunday worship, vague though it is, but he executes it poorly; we might say he has become incompetent in the practice of worship.

Forgetfulness and inattention are one of the first levels of corruptibility in a practice. They tend to creep into a person or community in a fairly innocuous way since it is impossible in every practice to attend to the fullness of intention and purpose. Habits allow us to carry forth a whole range of practices without analyzing every dimension every time we carry them out—we could not in fact practice if we were thinking about practice all the time. And, yet forgetfulness and inattention, when left unattended, can erode the foundation of practice and we end up doing things and not knowing why, or cease practicing, as in honoring the Sabbath, because we have been so inattentive to the deeper meaning and beliefs of the practice.

Another kind of corruptibility comes from selfish intentions. We abuse practices, intentionally, for our own aim or purposes. We become duplicitous, acting in one way, and yet striving for a purpose that serves ourselves. For example, Sally goes to church each Sunday in order to be looked on by the other members as a good and upright person. She sits in the front row with full attention on the words and music, volunteers for committee work, and makes large gifts, proud that her name is near the top of the donor list. Sally is a competent member in terms of carrying out good acts, but her intentions are self-serving and immoral. She is caught in what John Cassian, the fourth-century spiritual teacher, calls vainglory: doing the right thing for the wrong reasons.

Pride is a further corrupting influence. According to Cassian, pride is doing the wrong thing for the wrong reasons. Pride is a disease of the soul in which a person places themselves above all others, even God, surpassing the boundaries of communal rules, laws, or disciplines because "I know what is best." Pride corrupts practices because it blinds a person from seeing what is good and true in a practice because they believe they know what is good and true. In a certain sense pride is rejection of the social and communal "rules" of a practice. I do not need to observe the Sabbath on Sunday because I know what is best for me.

The kinds of corruptibility discussed so far have focused on the individual, but there is also social and communal corruptibility. The individual may be a person of good intention and practice but is part of a system in which false, immoral, or evil has become part of the warp and woof of a practice. Rarely, in fact, can individuals escape the influence of the corruption of systems. Any system in which practices are embedded can be caught up in a set of false claims, incorporating certain interpretations, meanings, and values into practices that spur the conditions of oppression, suppression, and injustice. Consider table fellowship practices again. In Jesus' time, a Jewish person would be considered unclean or unfit if he ate and drank with persons considered to be sinful or unclean. The rules of table fellowship operated in such a way as to include those who were deemed acceptable and to exclude the unacceptable. The practice of table fellowship itself becomes imbued with a grammar, a set of assumptions, attitudes, and beliefs that become commonly accepted and practiced. The wicked way in which communities define the "other" as a nonperson, or less than human, or as inferior becomes lodged in practices of inclusion and exclusion. The Pharisee does not even "see" the woman.

Each of these three types of corruptibility is present in the practices of ministry. The sheer repetition of visiting the sick each week, or preaching on Sundays, or teaching a class each year creates the condition for inattentiveness and forgetfulness about what one is doing and why. The practice becomes a rote habit, repeated and executed, but slowly severed from its deeper meaning and engagement. Likewise, ministers face their own selfish motives: praise, rewards, and power are all part of the ecclesial systems in which ministers work. Of course there is nothing inherently wrong with wanting to be a good minister and to exercise ministry in a competent way so that others recognize a person's gifts and abilities.

The corrupting influence of vainglory and pride is that the self becomes the focus of the practice and others become the means by which the self is aided in its quest for glory and power. And, finally, ecclesial systems are not immune from corruption, both by their own making as well as the cultural and social systems of which they are a part. The debates over who can be a minister and who cannot demonstrate the ways in which beliefs, values, and assumptions about human persons are embedded in ecclesial practice and appear unchangeable because they have always been done this way.

Practice as Spiritual Exercise

In the Christian tradition spirituality generally refers to the ways in which persons strive to be in communion with God, to cultivate experience of God's presence, and to be changed in and through this relationship. Spirituality is the human mode of being attuned to the Spirit's movements. It can refer to the general way in which all human persons seek to live in relationship to a transcendent dimension of existence. Spirituality also refers more specifically to the intentional paths chosen by an individual and community that involve a commitment to a set of disciplines and practices as a means to be in union with God. The spiritual traditions of both Eastern and Western Christianity that were initiated by a founder or saint each defined methods and practices that they believed could turn a person away from sin and toward a life in Christ. The idea of "spiritual exercises," for example, comes from St. Ignatius of Loyola.

For much of Christianity the spiritual tradition and its practices was the privilege of the church's ministers, primarily ordained priests and women in religious communities. The spirituality of the layperson was shaped largely by participation in the church's sacraments and various devotional practices. As spiritual theology developed in the modern period, authors wrote treatises for those who had chosen a path of holiness above and beyond the ordinary path of Christian obligation. The idea that spirituality is for an elite religious group tended to enforce the notion that some are higher and holier, closer to God, most especially those who live a celibate life. But hierarchies of spiritual persons and practices gave way to the idea, articulated by the Protestant Reformers of the sixteenth century and embraced at the Second Vatican Council, that all Christians share the call to a life of holiness rooted in our baptismal call and identity. It is widely accepted that whatever one's vocation, spirituality is a way for Christians to conform their life to Christ and to grow in love and holiness by "repeated exercises" of prayer and devotion. Today the diversity of spiritual practices and traditions are readily available to all.

Do ministers, then, have their own spirituality? Is there a spiritual practice that should be "exercised" by ministers? Rather than try to identify particular spiritual practices for ministers, I want to discuss approaches to spiritual practice that nurture the practice of ministry. Each minister will need to find the particular exercises that best express these approaches, but I think some form of both is necessary.

Many of us can make the mistake of thinking that to nurture a spiritual life means to get away to make a retreat, or to take up a meditation practice such as centering prayer or yoga, or to get up one hour earlier each day to pray. All of these are good practices, but they harbor a bias that spirituality is about escaping from daily realities to some silent, empty space where total peace can be experienced. There are times for retreat, but spirituality is not only about setting aside or apart as much as it is about living more intentionally and fully in the present moment, which for many of us means seeking the presence of God in common daily realities. In this case, it means seeking spiritual awareness in the practice of ministry, not apart from it.

There are two approaches to spiritual practice that are referred to as "kataphatic," the affirmative way, and "apophatic," the negative way. Both ways flow from ancient streams in Christianity and point out a deep paradox and truth: God is immanent, known through creation and the incarnation, and fully present to us within our very bodies; at the same time, God is wholly transcendent, separate and distinct from creation and human realities, not to be fully known or experienced in this life. Spiritual exercises that honor both kataphatic and apophatic awareness can help ministers balance this profound truth within their vocation and practice.

Ministry requires, first of all, kataphatic spiritual practice that focuses on the word spoken, the action taken, embodied presence, and discerned engagement. Kataphatic spirituality points to cultivating a deep intentionality of who I am and what I am doing by the words spoken and the action taken in the practices of ministry.

An affirmative spirituality calls the minister to discern how they will be present bodily, emotionally, and intellectually in their practice. It requires a mindfulness of practice: How will I speak these words at today's meetings? What can I communicate to a dying parishioner through my eyes? How can I help the staff think imaginatively about our next strategic plan? The kataphatic way seeks awareness of God in each situation and each person. Kataphatic prayer includes a frequent reading of the Scriptures; practices of mental and vocal prayer that give voice to the community's needs and concerns; and opening the imagination and senses to music, symbols, sacraments, and rituals in order to see and hear more deeply. Kataphatic spiritual exercises call forth the immanent dimensions of God's presence.

Ministry also requires apophatic spiritual practice that cultivates a sense of God's total otherness, the incomprehensible and ineffable of the divine holy mystery. Apophatic spirituality helps correct several misperceptions. First, it reminds us that even our conceptions of God are not God, and that nothing we do can fully explain who God is. Second, it helps ministers to not overidentify with God. The minister serves God's purposes, but is not God; the minister follows in Christ's footsteps to continue his ministry, but she or he is not Christ; the minister receives gifts of the Spirit for the sake of the community, but the gifts are not for their self-improvement or advancement. Third, apophatic practices remind the minister that God's presence in the community is in no way dependent on their actions. God is totally transcendent and other, one who cannot be cajoled, manipulated, or coerced. And fourth, apophatic ways remind ministers that they are fully human, fully disciple, not better or holier or closer to God than anyone else.

Apophatic spiritual practices in ministry have three dimensions. First, they require a self-emptying before God that moves beyond body, image, word, and thought. The apophatic tradition requires that one stands naked before God, going beyond what is seen, heard, and thought to a presence that cannot be named. Spiritual practices such as centering prayer, derived from the *Cloud of Unknowing*, provide a necessary balance to the kataphatic way in which image, word, and thought cultivate divine presence. Here, divine presence is experienced in the absence of these encounters.

The second dimension of apophatic spiritual practice is to purify intentions for action. The minister requires a "kenotic" self-emptying in order to make room for God's presence. Paul points to Christ's self-emptying, or kenosis, in which he took "the form of a slave" to humble himself in obedience, even to the cross (Phil 2:5-11). Kenosis is a forgetting of the self for the sake of the practice; it is not neglecting the self or placing the self above the situation. Rather, kenosis is living the paradox of emptying one's self of all false intention in order to speak God's Word. Purity of intention is cultivated by putting on the mind of Christ, as Paul says, in order that we might know ourselves rightly in relationship to God who is beyond all knowing.

Apophatic spirituality can also help ministers empty themselves of false intentions and poor practice. It is a way of intentionally examining the corruptions of heart and mind that infect ministry practice with dominance, pride, and control. Apophatic spiritual practices can guide ministers in recognizing these human tendencies and seeking God's healing presence for them.

The idea and study of practice sheds light on the interdependence and interconnectedness of human action and thought as bodily, personal, social, and historical realities. There is little that people do and think that is not deeply embedded in communities of practice. In theological anthropology practice expands our understanding of the human drama of God's invitation and human response. We can begin to see the ways in which God's practices of loving relationship draw humanity into a life of practice that becomes scripted onto persons and communities. We become what we practice, and if that practice is a response to God's dynamic embrace, our practices begin to participate in the redeeming practice of the world.

Sources for Further Reading

Bass, Dorothy C., ed. *Practicing our Faith: A Way of Life for a Searching People.* San Francisco, CA: Jossey-Bass, 1997.

———. *Receiving the Day: Christian Practices for Opening the Gift of Time.* San Francisco, CA: Jossey-Bass, 2000.

Beaudoin, Tom. *Witness to Dispossession: The Vocation of Post-modern Theologian.* Maryknoll, NY: Orbis Books, 2008.

Bernstein, Richard J. *Praxis and Action: Contemporary Philosophies of Human Activity.* Philadelphia: University of Pennsylvania Press, 1971.

Bourdieu, Pierre. *Outline of a Theory of Practice*. New York: Cambridge University Press, 1977.

Eiesland, Nancy L. *The Disabled God: Toward a Liberatory Theology of Disability*. Nashville, TN: Abingdon Press, 1994.

Funk, Mary Margaret. *Humility Matters for Practicing the Spiritual Life*. New York: Continuum, 2005.

Heitink, Gerben. *Practical Theology: History, Theory and Action Domains*. Grand Rapids, MI: Wm. B. Eerdmans, 1993.

Long, Thomas G. *Testimony: Talking Ourselves into Being Christian*. San Francisco, CA: Jossey-Bass, 2004.

Long, Thomas G., and Leonora Tubbs Tisdale, eds. *Teaching Preaching as a Christian Practice*. Louisville, KY: Westminster John Knox Press, 2008.

McInerny, Ralph. *Aquinas on Human Action: A Theory of Practice*. Washington, DC: The Catholic University of America Press, 1992.

Osmer, Richard R. *Practical Theology: An Introduction*. Grand Rapids, MI: Wm. B. Eerdmans, 2008.

Paulsell, Stephanie. *Honoring the Body: Meditations on a Christian Practice*. San Francisco, CA: Jossey-Bass, 2002.

Tilley,Terrence W. *Inventing Catholic Tradition*. Maryknoll, NY: Orbis Books, 2001.

Volf, Miroslav, and Dorothy C. Bass, eds. *Practicing Theology: Beliefs and Practices in Christian Life*. Grand Rapids, MI: Wm. B. Eerdmans, 2002.

Chapter 6

Learning to Practice Ministry

I have been developing a theology of vocation around two main concepts: the idea of the Spirit's charisms and practice. Vocation is a calling that addresses the whole of life—who I am, what I do, and how I live. Leaving aside the question of lifelong commitments in marriage, single life, or celibacy, I have examined charism and practice in relationship to questions of what I do and who I am. I have also left aside an exploration of other vocations that disciples are called to live, but I think the basic framework of charism and practice can be applied to the many forms of service that disciples pursue in work and volunteering. In fact, there is a growing literature on professions and professional service that has helped inform my theology of vocation as charism and practice, and I would like to pursue some of those ideas in this chapter.

In research on graduate-level professional education in the United States, scholars at the Carnegie Foundation are examining the pedagogies, or methods of teaching, that different professions employ to educate students in the professional practice of a given field. In comparative studies of law, engineering, nursing, medicine, and ministry, the professions train people in what William Sullivan calls the three apprenticeships: the cognitive apprenticeship, which focuses on developing knowledge and cultivating habits of mind; the practical apprenticeship, which focuses on habits of practice; and the moral apprenticeship, which focuses on learning the values, ethical commitments, and personal responsibilities of the profession.

In chapter 4 I identified three charisms for each practice of ministry, a charism related to knowing, to doing, and to being, following the idea of the three apprenticeships. I do not think, of course, that the Spirit's charisms are limited to three, nor do I want to imply that each practice is constituted by only three charisms. Rather, I am using the three apprenticeships from professional education research to identify some of the basic, foundational aspects of ministry.

The practitioner, to practice thoughtfully and well, must have knowledge, capacities and skills for action, and virtue. If one aspect of knowing, being, or doing is missing, a practice can be thoughtless, inept, or dishonest. For example, a minister can know a great deal about either theology or educational theory but be unable to teach in effective ways that foster understanding. Or a minister may be skilled in oration from the pulpit but only want a crowd to listen and adore them. Another minister might be honest, patient, and kind but unable to listen to the sick or counsel the depressed by offering them a message of understanding and hope.

Professional capacity, then, is not focused on one part of the self but on integrating knowing, doing, and being into one's practice. In any profession, this does not happen automatically or only by obtaining a graduate-level degree from a university. It is initiated and formed in and through education and practice within a community of practitioners that promotes ongoing learning, skill development, and self-formation.

This is true of ministry as well. As I stated in chapter 2, charisms are gifts that rarely come perfectly formed and ready for action. They usually come as small as a seed, to use Jesus' metaphor, and they need a great deal of healthy soil and tending to become fully mature (Mark 4:3-9). Another metaphor for this type of gift might be children's toys, the kind that require assembly, usually by a parent or adult. In our family, these gifts came in large boxes, with pieces of all shapes and sizes, and long detailed instructions requiring hours of frustrating work to assemble. The gift was opened, but it took a long time to finally receive it in a form with which we could actually play. Perhaps charisms are similar. They are gifts we receive, but they are not put together in a way that we can practice them in a full and competent way. The gift has to be constructed, usually through some frustration, patience, trial and error, and paying attention; we often need the help of others in both constructing and learning to use the gift.

In looking at ministry through the lens of professional practice, I want to explore the following questions in this chapter: What is a profession and how can we understand ministry as a profession? Like many professions, ministry is highly specialized, but is this a good development or not? How can we understand specialization in relationship to a theology of charisms: do ministers receive charisms for all the practices of ministry or only some? How do ministers learn their profession over time? Finally, what does it mean to be a wise and prudent practitioner?

Professional Practice

In addition to the definitions of practice noted in the previous chapter, the dictionary includes another entry: "to be professionally engaged."[1] The root meaning of "profession" is to "profess," which includes to "testify on behalf of," "stand for," and "avow."[2] Each profession consists of members who make a public commitment to be and to do for others through a particular service. At the heart of a profession is a covenant that both defines and constrains the professional, determining what they can and cannot do for another. A profession requires a public commitment that functions as a contract between the profession that promises to "stand for" something and the society's acceptance and acknowledgement of the profession's legitimacy and service. For example, in the United States, attorneys take an oath to uphold the Constitution and to represent their clients fairly and justly. They are expected to work for the rights and interests of their clients and to uphold the law in doing so.

Christian ministry is a profession that requires its members to profess a commitment to serve an ecclesial community, to represent that community and its members, and to conduct themselves in a way consistent with the religious claims of the group. This commitment is ritualized in the tradition of ordaining ministers. And even though religious leaders from every tradition vow to lead and serve a particular community, there is public and social recognition of the profession and some common understanding of what ministers do and why. In other words, it is important that ministry, like other professions in a pluralistic society, be seen in terms of a broader public commitment of service that demands responsibility and accountability. When religious leaders break their professional vows by financial corruption, inappropriate sexual relationships, or other abuses of power, the society judges their behavior harshly as both immoral and hypocritical. Some religious communities are shocked by "outsiders" judging their leaders. But harsh public censor

---

[1] *Merriam-Webster's Collegiate Dictionary*, 11th ed., s.v. "practice."

[2] William F. May, *Beleaguered Rulers: The Public Obligation of the Professions* (Louisville, KY: Westminster John Knox Press, 2001),14.

of ministers' sins is a sign that the public has certain expectations of ministers and that such public trust can be broken.

Professions share several common characteristics. They offer a service to society based on a special body of knowledge combined with competence in skill. Each profession is based on a moral commitment to serve the common good. Professions are communal and social as well, and they organize themselves in associations and societies to further educate and uphold standards of excellence.

Each profession is identified by a particular body of knowledge, what William May refers to as "esoteric knowledge," which distinguishes them from people outside the profession. Doctors learn about the body and medicine; lawyers about the Constitution, laws, and courts; and clergy learn about sacred texts, rituals, and traditions. A professional is expected to have a deep and extensive knowledge upon which society can depend. People outside a profession are generally not expected to know what the professional knows. A social worker does not know how to conduct surgery, nor does the surgeon understand how to treat abused children. The special body of knowledge acquired by a professional is one part of the professional's social contract: they can be expected to know things, which others can rely on, in their service.

In the modern period in Western countries professionals acquire knowledge primarily through forms of higher education. Prior to modern universities, most professions were learned through apprenticeships under a professional who belonged to a guild that granted a credential to a student when he or she mastered the knowledge and practice of the profession. Most professions today require extensive education in a knowledge base for their practice, with science and scientific ways of knowing as the predominate models in universities.

Ministry has followed a similar path and most denominations in North America require a master of divinity degree from an accredited seminary for ordination. Training for ministry in the university setting has had both positive and negative effects on theological education. Positively, the university setting has demanded that religious scholarship and theology be open to multiple forms of knowledge and interact with a world of ideas. Negatively, theology has been persuaded at times to be too scientific and rational, to value abstractness and objectivity, and to maintain distance from the object being studied. But this is not the kind of knowing for which theology is best engaged, and it is not what is best for ministry. In a major study on how ministry is taught, the authors of *Educating Clergy* note:

> Unlike the abstract and theoretic formulations of the modern sci-
> ences, religious understanding is deeply and inescapably connected
> to identity and meaning. It carries import for how one understands
> one's life, including powerful implications of a normative kind for
> how one ought to live. In many of its traditional forms, religious
> knowledge has argued that one can understand reality only by hav-
> ing the right stance toward it: that existential attunement, or grace,
> is a condition as well as a result of knowledge. That is, the question
> of God, although deeply cognitive, cannot be approached on the
> model of empirical science. . . . [I]t demands a stance different from
> that required by science. It requires engagement as well as critical
> distance.[3]

Ministry is distinctive from other professions in terms of what it knows and the ways of knowing. In terms of knowing, I identified the following charisms in chapter 5: A minister receives gifts for the knowledge of: the Christian faith, tradition, and Scriptures, the historical context, and ways of interpretation for today's context; human experience in relationship to human sin, brokenness, and suffering as well as joy, healing, and reconciliation; worship and prayer, particularly rituals, symbols, and sacraments; the theological and ethical teachings on social issues; the vision for the church's mission and systems to administer its resources. Again, a gift for knowledge does not mean that a person automatically knows this body of knowledge. Learning the tradition and contemporary thought requires years of reading, studying, questioning, and thinking. The charism is the gift for the desire as well as the ability to learn and understand.

The particular knowledge that is unique to ministry is called practical theological interpretation. Richard Osmer describes this task as learning to engage four questions in the context of ministry: What is going on? Why is this going on? What ought to be going on? And how might we respond? The first question asks the minister to "read their context." Ministers need to develop the capacity to interpret situations, contexts, and the people in them. Interpreting situations requires learning how to read, inquire, research, and understand the historical, social, cultural, and personal contexts in which people live. Ministers must become wise interpreters of a range of human reality and experiences, from birth to

---

[3] Charles R. Foster, Lisa E. Dahill, Lawrence A. Golemon, Barbara Wang Tolentino, *Educating Clergy: Teaching Practices and Pastoral Imagination* (San Francisco, CA: Jossey-Bass, 2006), 4.

death, and offer religious insight that gives meaning and purpose to human lives. They also learn to interpret what they see God doing in the situation. The first step Osmer calls the descriptive-empirical task because it requires the ability to gather "information that helps us discern patterns and dynamics in particular episodes, situations or contexts."[4]

Understanding what is going on leads to the second question, why? In this task the minister needs to step back and explore various theories that help explain the dynamics of a situation (e.g., cultural studies, sociology, psychology, family systems, economics, philosophy, religious studies, and theology). In addition to learning theoretical models that shed light on what is happening and why, the minister must respond in the situation. They have to ask from a theological point of view, what ought to be going on here? The normative task of ministry involves searching for God's presence and activity and the faithful human response, examining relevant ethical principles and guidelines, and exploring Christian practices from the past and present. The fourth question to be explored in practical theological thinking is, how might we respond? The minister thinks through the strategies and actions that are possible to achieve a desired outcome or goal.

In order to explore answers to these questions, ministers are interpreters of texts as well as contexts. Religious texts come in many forms, including the sacred texts canonized as Scripture (which include a variety of genres), theological writings in the form of church council decrees, and doctrinal formulations, as well as liturgies, prayers, music, art, architecture, and spiritual writings. Learning to interpret a tradition requires knowledge of the historical context of written and visual texts, but also the norms of interpretation held by a community over time, which are never neutral in religious communities. All facets of interpretation presume theological perspective, a way of understanding God in relationship to the religious community's identity and practices in the past, present, and future. Knowledge of theology, history, ethics, and ministry is not an end in itself, but serves to inform the minister's discernment of the most fitting response in each situation. According to Osmer and other practical theologians, the cognitive habits of mind, or the way of thinking, in ministry is distinctive because it involves the complex interplay of divine reality in relationship to human existence across vast historical and contemporary contexts.

---

[4] Richard R. Osmer, *Practical Theology: An Introduction* (Grand Rapids, MI: Wm. B. Eerdmans, 2008), 4.

Professionals know about something but they also have knowledge about how to do something. They gain knowledge in the foundational ideas or theories of the profession, but they also must gain knowledge in relationship to the skills and capacities—what they do. The cardiac surgeon learns how the human heart functions, but she also must learn how to perform a surgery. In medicine, this know-how is central to the education of nurses and doctors. Teaching and learning happen at the bedside of patients in a hospital in order that knowledge about and know-how come together in practice. But ministers do not require the same kind of "technological skills that enable them to alter the physical conditions of life" in the way that doctors or engineers or architects must learn. "The clergy's area of expertise lies not in physical or information systems, but in the world of social practices structured by shared meanings, purposes, and loyalties."[5] What is central to theological education for ministry is learning to know the Scriptures, the tradition, and its theological beliefs and arguments in order to acquire skills and competence in teaching, preaching, and the other practices. The very heart of the minister's work is to form and sustain a community of disciples, which is not value-free or objective work. It is deeply formative, transformative, and political. The ways to do this work, the practical knowledge of know-how, are deeply important and are learned in and through engagement in multiple learning contexts.

In terms of doing, the charisms to embody and execute a practice include the capacities: to speak clearly and persuasively to foster understanding of the mind and conversion of the heart; to listen attentively and offer guidance, healing, sustenance, and reconciliation; to preside and lead with gracious presence; to identify human needs and organize resources to respond; and to manage and administer the community's resources to serve its mission. As gifts, the charisms for skills and capacities require ongoing education: one can learn better and more effective ways of speaking, listening, guiding, and administering. The gift points to the potential to be developed through practice.

In addition to cognitive and practical apprenticeships, professionals learn the values, morals, and public commitments of a profession. Many professions are learning today that they cannot teach pure science in a value-neutral way. Not only does science have values, but the science-based professions are filled with normative perspectives connected to

---

[5] William M. Sullivan, "Introduction," in Foster et al., *Educating Clergy*, 8.

the public good. Do we want to train engineers, for example, to respect the environment? Do we want compassionate nurses and doctors who understand suffering? Do we want ministers who are committed to living the life of faith they are called to represent and promote?

An essential hallmark of professions is that they are altruistic. They exist to serve some human need and contribute to the common good. Professionals are not to practice for self-gain, promotion, or only financial advance. Concern for the well-being of the other is a hallmark of professions. When we go to a professional for help or assistance we expect them to give their attention and expertise to our situation wholeheartedly. This is part of the covenant of the professional: they have special knowledge and expertise that they are willing to give on behalf of others and people can trust that a service will be rendered on their behalf. But when the social contract is broken, even by a few, the profession's public image can be damaged. Increasing exposure of racial profiling, for example, has led to widespread suspicion of the police in some communities. They are not viewed as having the community's welfare in mind when they unfairly target, arrest, and jail innocent people because of race. Professional covenants can become fragile and ministry has also witnessed that repeated acts of misconduct by people in the profession erode public trust and lead to public cynicism.

Ministers are expected to be especially altruistic because they teach about moral principles and rules, such as charity and mercy, and they hold people in their communities accountable to high moral standards. On one level, ministers must continue to be attentive to their own practices of discipleship, to the ways they embody their faith in what they do, how they live, and who they become. They need to attend to the ways in which they are following, worshiping, witnessing, forgiving, and being a neighbor, prophet, and steward. In addition they must be open to being formed through the practices of ministry in order that they foster attentiveness to the ways of God within the realities of human life, the contemporary contexts in which people live, and the resources they draw on within the tradition. Ministers who are formed over time in the life of discipleship and ministry develop capacities for attentive watching and listening to God's ways within the community of disciples, the world, and their own lives.

In terms of the moral dimension of the self, the virtues related to the practice of ministry arise from the charisms of humility, empathy, compassion, adoration and awe, mercy and justice, attentiveness, and generosity. The list of virtues, of course, goes on and on, and there are numerous virtues that become part of a person's being and identity because of the kind of life they lead and the way they undertake their practice. As foundational virtues for the practices, I see these as essential for the minister but there are many more virtues that can be listed such as thoughtfulness, gratitude, perseverance, patience, openness, vigilance, integrity, imagination, humor, hospitality, joy, candor, cooperativeness, and so on.

Finally, the practice of professionals is a social and communal reality. Professionals throughout history have organized into groups to oversee that practitioners uphold the highest standards. Professions can train their members or establish criteria for education, monitor the quality of services being offered, and regulate and discipline those who do not uphold the standards and rules. Professional associations serve to advance the knowledge base, skill level, and moral commitments of its members. In ministry, denominations and churches oversee the development and formation of ministry through seminary education and forms of continuing education after graduation. In addition, numerous professional organizations uphold the standards for excellence in particular practices of ministry. Many organizations are based in particular denominations, such as the National Association of Pastoral Musicians, which serves the Catholic community. Others are ecumenical and work with ministers from a variety of denominations, such as the National Association of Church Business Administrators or the Association of Professional Chaplains. Increasing professional standards are good for ministry, both in terms of its commitment to serve particular faith communities but also in its efforts to serve the common good.

Specialization in Ministry

But increased professionalization points to another phenomenon: specialization. Specialization in ministry is so commonplace that we hardly notice it. Like many professions that are shaped by university standards of education and research, ministry in Protestant and Catholic settings has become a highly specialized field in congregations as well as in schools, hospitals, social service agencies, and universities. Many large congregations employ staff to oversee some specific aspect of parish life such as faith formation, liturgy, music, youth ministry, social justice and outreach, pastoral care, and business administration. Advertisements seek ministers qualified in each of these roles and it seems rare that a minister trained in one "area" crosses over to apply for a position in another. Generally, a minister with ten years of experience in faith formation would not be considered qualified for a position in liturgy. Or a person with fifteen years of experience leading a parish might be seen as unqualified to lead a campus ministry. This phenomenon can be true for both ordained and nonordained ministers.

Why has specialized ministry developed and expanded? First, the body of knowledge related to all areas of ministry has exploded over the past century. The status of ministry as a profession, developed according to university standards and academic criteria, has enhanced each practice of ministry as an area of study. Some practices, especially catechesis, liturgy, pastoral care, and preaching, exist as their own academic disciplines in the university, with doctoral-level education, professional organizations, and journals aimed at researchers. Each has a theoretical base that draws on biblical and theological sources as well as the social sciences and philosophy. For example, liturgical studies draws heavily on anthropological research about ritual, homiletics turns to communication theory, and pastoral care has had a long-standing conversation with several branches of psychology.

In addition to disciplinary expertise, professional organizations for practitioners have expanded, each with national and regional conferences, journals, and magazines. Take the field of Catholic catechesis, for instance, which has several journals for practitioners (*Catechist, Liturgical Catechesis*), national organizations (National Conference for Catechetical Leadership, National Catholic Young Adult Ministry Association, National Federation of Catholic Youth Ministry), national certification standards for lay ecclesial ministers, and opportunities for advanced degrees at a number of Catholic universities across the country. The same can be said for many other church communities.

For all that is positive about the expanding knowledge base, there are several consequences to specialization that can be perilous for ministry. First, specialization can lead to narrow understandings of ministerial identity and vocation. Ministers can overly identify with one practice of ministry because they are hired for a particular role in a particular context. A catechist, prison chaplain, or school administrator may come to view their particular practice as so preeminent it becomes disconnected from the other practices over time. Because the role and setting strongly determine the practice, ministers may fail to see the ways in which catechetical ministry or pastoral care encompasses all aspects of ministry, not just specialization in a particular area. Does the catechist understand his or her ministry to include pastoral care with parishioners and students, and does the chaplain take time to catechize a hospital patient and family? Further, how does the liturgist play a role in catechizing the parish, and how is preaching related to prophecy and the administration of the community's resources?

Specialized knowledge leads to the sense that one's expertise lies in a particular area but is limited in other areas. We see this in the profession of medicine where the orthopedic surgeon who specializes in knees will not (or cannot) answer a question about neck pain. Both doctors are in orthopedic medicine but only treat one joint. But do we want ministers whose primary identity is with one aspect of ministry and not with ministry as a whole? "I'm a preacher. Go see the administrator about that question." Or, "I'm a chaplain; you need a liturgist to plan the service." (I once heard a group of ministry students say they would not plan a liturgy because none of them were liturgists.) A minister may feel that "I cannot encroach on the other areas of ministry because I lack that expertise," or may tend to embrace other areas of ministry through the lens of their own specialty: "As a catechist, I *teach* about liturgy and social justice."

In the worst cases, specialization leads to competition between ministers—office space, church resources, the attention of the pastor, or the priorities of the church council. Congregations also can become overly identified with one aspect of their ministry—the church with great liturgy but an underdeveloped social justice program, or the social justice parish with little or no catechesis, or the community with great preaching but little pastoral care for its members.

When a person is called to ministry is it the case that they are called to leadership in all six areas of ministry or to just one or two practices? Do they receive all the charisms or only some? A minister's calling is to the leadership of disciples; they commit themselves in public service to the whole of discipleship—leading disciples to be followers, worshipers, witnesses, forgivers, neighbors, prophets, and stewards. Likewise, they are called to serve as ministers in relationship to the whole of ministry in whatever setting or role they assume: the liturgist is also catechist, the pastoral counselor is also prophet, and the administrator leads the community in prayer. Every minister meets the disciple as disciple—not some part of discipleship. In other words, the catechist is not meant to relate to the disciple solely as follower, or the pastoral caregiver to the forgiver and neighbor.

Ministers do not receive one charism or the charisms for one practice. Rather, it seems that most receive a constellation of gifts. A person discerning a call to ministry discerns the whole of ministry and their gifts and capacities within the practices of ministry. Teaching, for example, may be a person's primary charism, but gifts of pastoral care and leading worship are also apparent. If, however, a minister has responsibility for the community's catechesis, they are called to lead that ministry in relationship to all the practices of ministry, whether they have received the charisms or not. But is that possible and realistic?

It is the case that ministers do not receive all the gifts for the six practices of ministry. One person is a good preacher but not as well equipped for accompanying the dying; another has gifts for administering institutions but is not as skilled at teaching; another has the gifts for teaching children but cannot manage an organization. The community needs ministers to serve in roles where their charisms are best expressed, and that means many ministers are called to serve in specialized roles and will develop their capacities in some areas of ministry and not others.

To say that ministers are called to understand, practice, and embody the six practices of ministry in their work, and that they have charisms for some but not all practices of ministry, has important implications for how we think about ministry as a communal practice. Ministry is practiced within a community of practitioners to ensure that both happen. Only by working collaboratively can ministers on a congregational staff, for instance, ensure that the practices of ministry are not slotted into defined roles or titles, but are present in each person's practice and "area." In circumstances where a particular minister is not well equipped or capable in a certain area, they work with others to ensure that the fullness of ministry is expressed in their area. They can both work to develop the skills in their own practice and they can invite others to share their gifts. For example, the preacher identifies those with the gifts for visiting the dying to accompanying him or her on their visits; the administrator seeks help from good teachers when called upon to explain the budget; the chaplain seeks a liturgist to help plan a funeral service. In this way, ministers together ensure that all aspects of ministry are present in the community for the sake of the community's discipleship. The need to collaborate is a theological demand: the six practices are rarely fully formed and expressed in one person alone but the Spirit ensures that the charisms are present for the practices within the body. Even for ordained ministers, who are called to preside over the entire community, there should not be the expectation that they have received all the charisms for ministry, but rather that they have the gift to coordinate and lead the various charisms and practices of ministry for the community's life together.

Learning Ministry over Time

The title of this section is taken from a book chapter by Christian Scharen, a Lutheran pastor and professor of liturgy and ministry.[6] He writes about the "longer arc of learning" that is required for ministers within and beyond seminary education by using a developmental learning framework based on the work of Hubert Dreyfus and Stuart Dreyfus. The Dreyfus brothers examine how people acquire skill in particular professional practices such as airplane pilots, chess players, and military commanders. They describe how experiential learning in the context of practice occurs, and they identify five stages in which a professional moves from being a novice to advanced beginner to competent, and with further reflective practice some practitioners move on to be proficient and expert. The first three stages are marked by formal training in school and the early years of professional practice when practice is closely related to learning and applying theories in a process of deliberate rational thinking. The latter two stages are a kind of practice that transcends deliberate thought that is mostly intuitive and known from experience.

Their model is a helpful heuristic tool in pointing to how various levels of ability, knowledge, and virtue emerge over time in and through practice. The model is helpful in drawing our attention to what is common among all practitioners as they learn. Nevertheless, models such as the Dreyfus' can mistakenly appear to be a kind of rule book or step-by-step process. Rather, it is descriptive of how practitioners in a variety of fields learn over time. Learning is a complex matter and it happens for each of us in different ways, at different paces, and in different contexts. Part of good teaching is recognizing variability of learning styles, but it is also part of good learning: students gain awareness into the settings and circumstances in which they learn best and each person comes to negotiate the fluidity, ambiguity, and anxiety of learning new skills and ideas in their own way.

In teaching ministry, I see students with different ranges of academic ability but also different levels of practice-ability. I see students with varying degrees of integration between what they know and do and who they are. And because the six practices of ministry are different and distinctive, I have taught entering ministry students who are competent in some areas of ministry, and in other areas they are novices or advanced beginners. In some ecclesial traditions, a person can serve as a minister

---

[6] Christian Scharen, "Learning Ministry over Time: Embodying Practical Wisdom," in *For Life Abundant*, 265–88.

with little to no professional preparation, which is often the case for lay or nonordained ministers. And in some churches a person can be ordained with little formal education. This means that seminary classrooms are filled with students with varying levels of experience and knowledge related to ministry. To employ the Dreyfus model in reflecting on ministry, then, it is important to remember that each person embodies a mixture of stages across a range of practices, and no one person goes through the stages in a simple step-by-step fashion. As noted in the previous section, most ministers will be attracted to the practices of ministry in which they discern that they have charisms and capacities.

A novice is generally a person who has little experience in the practice of ministry, which does not mean that they come to theological education with no understanding of ministry. If they have been raised in a church, involved in various ministries as teens or young adults, they have already been shaped by communities of practice. They know something about ministry by observing ministers and pastors. They have formed assumptions, opinions, and impressions about ministry, and they have some sense that they might be called to serve in such a role. In addition, there are students who have not been raised or formed in an ecclesial community, but they have been formed in some communities of practice, with some type of leadership, from which they too have formed impressions and beliefs about leadership and ministry. In other words, students come with a range of experiences and assumptions about ministry, but the novice student has yet to practice ministry in terms of either leading an area of its ministry or leading a community in shaping its life together.

I have seen two kinds of novices in graduate theological education. The first is the novice who has little experience in ministry, and the second type of novice is the person who has experience and perhaps training in one practice of ministry but little experience or knowledge in another. For example, Katie entered full-time graduate studies with a bachelor degree in human services and a minor in theology and a year of service in a volunteer organization. She immersed herself in learning the practices of interpretation of texts in Bible, history, theology, and ethics courses. In addition, she began to learn something of the practice of ministry in courses on catechesis, pastoral care, and social ministry. In her studies and field education, she began to explore issues in young adult ministries, particularly in the local Catholic diocese, and found there was little compelling programming being offered. She was concerned for the church and for members her age that were not connecting to the faith tradition in a vital way. In a capstone integration course, she designed a yearlong educational and social program to provide more comprehensive and in-depth formation for young adults. Upon graduation she was hired by a Franciscan community to lead this program and to build an intentional community in one of their houses. In many ways, Katie entered graduate school a novice. She had not led a young adult ministry and knew little about the issues until she began to read, research, and interview young adults and young adult ministers.

Regina is another kind of novice. She came to the Master of Divinity program with many years of training and experience in liturgy and music. She had no education or experience in pastoral care, except leading the music at funeral liturgies. She was curious if there were ways she could incorporate her liturgical and musical experience into pastoral care. Throughout the MDiv program this question pursued her; she studied the role of music in pastoral care in history courses, she found a clinical pastoral education site where she could use music, and in her final semester she designed a program for parish liturgical ministers to discern if they had a call to work with the sick and the dying. In many ways, Regina was a novice in the practice of pastoral care, but through continued study and practice, she gained basic knowledge and experience to enable her to integrate pastoral care and liturgy and music together in her practice.

Novices are beginners. They often want to learn the basic rules and guidelines for a practice: What is the best way to conduct a parish meeting? Deliver a funeral homily? Visit a sick church member? Katie was interested in researching the best young adult programs and how to apply their ideas in a local situation. Regina initially wanted to figure out what kinds of music are appropriate to play for the sick and dying, including what instruments and songs. At times students can be embarrassed about their novice status and apologize for their questions as if everyone else knows what to do except them. But why? Novices do not generally know and the only way they will come to know is by learning and doing. Basic skills and knowledge are necessary to teach and learn and cannot be skipped over.

Novices depend on teachers to introduce them to ways of thinking about faith and practice, to teach them the central theories in a field, and to engage them in basic elements of practice. In the beginning novices depend strongly on theories and existing models and use them as guides and rule books. Novices need experiences in the classroom as well as the field to put models, theories, and methods developed by experts in the field to work. As professor of pastoral care Bonnie Miller-McLemore says, "We send students to the field to interview, observe, and otherwise encounter the 'real,' as well as to witness, report on, and learn from actual practitioners."[7] Learning a practice means practicing it over and over again. She writes that the "unspoken rule or litany" is "experience the practice, practice it, tell about it, ask questions about it, read about it, write about it, practice it, do it, empower others to do it."[8] Professor of liturgy John Witvleit states that the beginning practitioner, whether in music, sports, or ministry, has to learn the basic "scales" of their practice: "The key to success is repeated, disciplined rehearsal of key skills. . . . As any veteran athlete or musician knows, these drills and scales are a critical part of the work, an activity from which one never graduates."[9]

One problem in theological education is that teaching and learning about basic skills or know-how appears to be about merely technique and functions. What critics often fail to see is that novices need the "hints, tips, and rules of thumb" of a practice, not because they constitute full ministerial practice, but because that is where practice begins. As Miller-McLemore writes, "When rules of thumb are deeply connected to the beauty of richly embodied, theologically responsible practice, they play a needed (even if limited) role in helping students move toward practical theological wisdom."[10] As she points out, there are better and worse ways to stand when speaking, to enter a hospital room, or to elevate the plate and cup during the eucharistic prayer. "One may feel artificial and forced in making these moves at first, but over time, as one experiments with particular gestures and phrases, practices them over and over, and considers their theological implications, they can become a more reliable and authentic part of one's own pastoral repertoire."[11]

The novice moves to an advanced beginner when they begin to practice, trying on the theories and methods they have been learning in context. For many novice students this happens in supervised ministry settings during their education or in their first few years of ministry. It was not hard to see both Katie and Regina become advanced beginners as they began testing their ideas in field education and clinical pastoral

---

[7] Bonnie J. Miller-McLemore, "Practical Theology and Pedagogy: Embodying Theological Know-How" in *For Life Abundant*, 179.

[8] Ibid., 178.

[9] John Witvleit, "Teaching Worship as a Christian Practice," in Bass and Dykstra, *For Life Abundant*, 140.

[10] Bonnie Miller-McLemore, "Practical Theology and Pedagogy," 180.

[11] Ibid.

education. They began to know more once they had to minister to young adults, in Katie's case, and, in Regina's case, to play music for the sick and dying. The advanced beginner tries on the new role, is able to assess the situation, and begins to make decisions about how to proceed.

In addition to book and field learning, the novice and advanced beginner have identity-forming experiences when people recognize a student as *minister*. The identity of minister is oftentimes mirrored back to the student for the first time in supervised settings. Parishioners greet the student as minister, chaplain, teacher, or student pastor. This often happens in clinical pastoral education settings when a student is wearing a nameplate with the title "chaplain." It does not say "novice" or "advanced beginner" or "rookie"; it says "chaplain," which is how people respond to them, with the expectations of who a chaplain is and what a chaplain does. Recognition by others of a particular role and identity is itself a formative moment and requires a student to begin to embrace the responsibilities and expectations of a new position. This is the case despite the fact that many students feel as though they barely know what to do or how to do it when they enter a congregation or a hospital room for the first time.

Annette had seventeen years of teaching experience in a grade school when she entered ministry studies. She began discovering different areas of parish ministry that began to intrigue her. One summer she served as an intern in a local parish. Her supervisor was the minister of care and visited people in the hospital, shut-ins, and those who lived in long-term care facilities. After a few weeks accompanying her on the visits, Annette took over. She visited three parishioners on a memory-loss unit. She brought them Communion, performing the rite exactly as she was taught in liturgy class, but she raced off the ward as fast as possible when she was finished. She had no idea how to be in communion with these parishioners. Fortunately, she had enough experience as a teacher and had a wise mentor who was able to help her identify how she felt (scared and uncertain of how to interact with the residents), what she needed to know (about the physical, emotional, and social effects of dementia), and what to say and do (the "know-how" of caregivers who serve those with severe memory loss). After graduation, she left teaching and is now a pastoral associate in a large parish.

The best learning situation for the advanced beginner is to have a strong mentor or supervisor who practices with him or her and whose practice he or she respects. An advanced beginner can both observe the mentor in practice and be observed. Mentors can become dialogue partners, explaining their own thinking behind their practice, as well as guiding a student-minister in their own performance and skill development. The advanced beginner is very conscious of their actions and those around them, often comparing and critiquing themselves to others. The advanced beginner needs to learn from good practice, even if at the outset they often mimic the practice of others.

It is common for anxiety and self-doubt to be prominent for the advanced beginner, especially in new and unfamiliar situations in which they must perform. Heidi Neumark, a Lutheran pastor, tells of her experience in field education in which the pastor told her to start a youth club. "There was only one problem. I had no experience. I had received no training for this sort of thing in seminary. I was shy. . . . What would I say? What would I do? What if no one wanted to talk to me? And the bottom line—what if I failed? Did I mention that I didn't know anybody on Beulah Street?"[12] She spoke with the pastor about her uncertainty, and he said, "How can you fail? Whatever you do won't be so bad as doing nothing." She admitted that "he had said what I needed to hear" and she launched into the ministry developing the Beulah Street Bunch.

The key moments of learning at this point often come through missteps, mistakes, and failures. If a student has a wise guide, such moments become opportunities for further learning in new areas, exploring what might be better moves to take in similar situations. Rick Osmer entered ministry as a pastor of a small-town Presbyterian church. He entered the position enthusiastic about Christian education and started a Sunday school program, attracting young families with children to the church. Excited about the possibilities of "becoming known as a church with a future and not just a past," he installed a swing set for the children next to a covered picnic area where people gathered for food and conversation. Two weeks later when he came to work, the swing set was gone, actually moved to the back of the church and cemented into place. He writes, "I wish that at least one class of my theological education had given me the knowledge and skills to make sense of what I was experiencing. I realize, in ministry, experience is one of our most important teachers. But experiences like this one in which lives and years of work are at stake can leave us bewildered."[13] Situations such as Osmer's clash with the parishioner who moved the swing set are times of uncertainty

[12] Heidi B. Neumark, *Breathing Space: A Spiritual Journey in the South Bronx* (Boston, MA: Beacon Press, 2003), 22.
[13] Osmer, *Practical Theology*, 3.

and self-examination: How does it feel when I don't perform well or when I fail? How do I face adversity and conflict with people? What did I do wrong? Does this mean that I might not have a vocation to ministry? What could I do differently next time? What do I need to do in order to practice better in the future?

These experiences are crucial moments in which either a door into deeper more reflective practice opens, or a person is too afraid or intimidated and closes that door. The open door is inviting a person to learn something new, perhaps gaining new knowledge, or trying a different skill or approach. Ministers need to learn the practice of examining and assessing their abilities, both their strengths and where they need to grow. What can be startling for some advanced beginners is the realization that seminary did not teach them everything and that they are still "in school" in the sense that they need to keep learning, reading, researching, and understanding the situation and themselves. What many beginning ministers do not always understand is that the range of emotional reaction, which is often exhausting and confusing, is a normal part of launching into full-blown practice.

Perhaps one of the virtues that can emerge for the advanced beginner, in addition to humility, is the virtue of humor, the ability to laugh at oneself or to not take oneself too seriously. Heidi Neumark tells of another field education experience in a poor inner-city neighborhood. She was told to create a flyer for a Sunday school program and place it under every door in four twenty-one-story projects. She was told by her supervisor to wait until someone could accompany her, but Heidi became impatient and, confident in her "black shirt with its white clerical collar," she headed into the buildings, in August. She got stuck in the stairwell when the electricity went out. When she began sweating profusely she "pulled out the white collar tab and opened a few buttons." She is able to tell this story in a humorous way and invite us to laugh with her about losing her "pastoral identity" in the dark. She was eventually found by some children who helped her out of the building.[14]

To transition from seminary into full-time ministry, especially for those who find themselves newly ordained or in new roles, is to step into a new learning situation. David Wood argues that the "actual performance of ministry, in local congregations and in relation to mature practitioners, is how and where pastors begin to form pastoral identity." If a minister

---

[14] Neumark, *Breathing Spaces*, 21–23.

is to gain greater capacity in pastoral practice, they need "reflective, appreciative, critical engagement with congregational culture." The ministry setting is now the classroom, and it is important that advanced beginners find experienced practitioners as well as peers to be their teachers and classmates. Without sustained attention to learning in practice in the first few years of ministry, many people will face burnout, unnecessary conflict, ill health, and emotional upset. Wood writes that the "habits and practices instilled during the initial years of ministry have a shelf life that impacts one's pastoral practice for years to come."[15]

Competent ministry emerges when a minister has an array of experiences as well as knowledge and theories that they can use in thinking and acting as they approach both familiar and new situations. According to the Dreyfus model, this generally happens in the first two years of full-time practice after education is completed when a practitioner takes on the full identity, role, and responsibility of the profession. According to Patricia Benner who has studied nurses, "The competent stage of skill acquisition is typically a time of heightened planning for what are now more predictable immediate futures."[16] An educated, competent professional has had enough experience, and has learned from that experience, to predict situations better, to know what is important and what is less important, and to be able to discern better the particulars of a given situation and bring them into dialogue with more general information.

Johnny Ray Youngblood, an African-American minister at St. Paul's Church in the Bronx, hated seminary. It unraveled his faith and he questioned its relevance for how it would make him a better preacher. A teacher told him, "School will do for a preacher what a grinding stone will do for an ax."[17] He stayed on to graduate, but only found that entering ministry was far more intimidating than seminary. He found a mentor to serve under as an associate pastor and began to witness how "Reverend Jones put that real-world Jesus to work, and radically so, in government, economics, religion, and family. For a time, Reverend Youngblood modeled himself on his mentor down to his fondness for alliteration and

[15] David J. Wood, "Transition into Ministry: Reconceiving the Boundaries between Seminaries and Congregations," in *For Life Abundant*, 292.

[16] Patricia Benner, "Using the Dreyfus Model of Skill Acquisition to Describe and Interpret Skill Acquisition and Clinical Judgment in Nursing Practice and Education," *Bulletin of Science, Technology and Society* vol. 24, no. 3 (June 2004): 193.

[17] Samuel G. Freedman, *Upon This Rock: The Miracle of the Black Church* (New York: HarperCollins, 1993), 178.

his habit of touching his left hand to his temple. But with his own pulpit, at Saint Paul, he became his own preacher."[18] His story, told in the book *Upon This Rock*, demonstrates how a novice became an advanced beginner and grew to be a competent minister not only in preaching but also in pastoral care, vision, administration, and a highly successful social justice ministry that literally rebuilt the neighborhood through the construction of about two thousand homes called the Nehemiah Project.

Anxiety or fear is not as general and is more specific to situations. Both joy at good performance and sadness or remorse in poor performance are key emotional aspects of competence. Benner notes that "these emotional responses are the formative stages of aesthetic appreciation of good practice. These feelings of satisfaction and uneasiness with performance act as a moral compass that guides experiential ethical and clinical learning."[19] Heidi Neumark recalls returning to her congregation in the South Bronx after attending an urban ministry conference abroad: "I realized again how much I love being here and worshipping here and how privileged I am. . . . At Transfiguration, I don't feel that I am 'up front' and the congregation is 'out there,' even though our space reflects that arrangement. Instead, I feel a contrapuntal exchange of energy, back and forth, in and out, through and through, a power circling around the room. I used to be much stiffer when conducting worship, stiffer in general. The congregation has shaken me loose and made me shiver in places I didn't know were there. I am blessed."[20]

Competent ministers develop an ability to "think on their feet" as the theories, models, and methods they memorized move into the background, and their own experience-based knowledge comes more to the fore. Because a minister has more and more experience in various practices in different contexts, they have a more immediate sense of the needs and responses of people. This means the minister learns to identify choices, deliberate about them, think through the consequences of each in order to make a good choice. The minister has moved beyond knowing theories about church to being a leader of a church. They also move beyond finding the right program, to more authentic interactions with people.

I have known many competent ministers, and some are graduate students like Annette who come with years of experience, have a wealth

---

[18] Ibid., 184.
[19] Patricia Benner, "Using the Dreyfus Model," 194.
[20] Neumark, *Breathing Space*, 167.

of knowledge, and know what they are doing, but they also like new challenges. Chris is a competent youth minister with eight years of experience in a suburban parish. He leads a highly successful program that emphasizes spiritual, moral, and cognitive development of youth. He reads, attends conferences, and networks with other ministers. He evaluates his ministry and is not afraid to question his own practice. One aspect of his ministry, the annual mission trip, is especially successful, but he was not satisfied. With about 12 percent of the youth attending weeklong immersion experiences in either Mexico or an urban setting, he did not feel that the experience was leading to a lifelong commitment to social justice outside these special events. He was not searching for another program but for what would most connect young people to see social justice as intrinsic to their discipleship and how they could live a life of service each day. He was seeking for ways to call these young disciples to embrace their identity as prophets.

Competence is a key quality for the flourishing of charisms and basic skills. To be a competent professional in any field means that one has a sense of his or her responsibility, abilities, and how best to serve others. Many people maintain a level of high competence through much of their professional ministry practice. When a minister meets the limits of their practice and they desire to know and do more in future situations, they begin to strive toward proficiency and expertise. Moving to proficiency in the Dreyfus model requires more intentional learning and rigorous practice. It is exemplified in a different kind of thinking, emotional reaction, and identity.

Proficient practitioners think within practice differently. As Chris Scharen describes, "We act in skillful ways by using a less conscious 'knowing how' that depends on familiarity and experience." It is a kind of thinking "'without thinking,' intuitively drawing on 'know-how' that is the result of many similar experiences that now provide the mental backdrop for an immediate course of action in this current situation."[21] A proficient minister can recognize the features of a situation and pause to think about the various courses of action to take and choose an appropriate response. As a minister gains experience of thinking through situations along with gauging consequences and reactions, they grow more proficient in practice.

---

[21] Scharen, "Learning Ministry over Time," 284–85.

Benner notes that the proficient practitioner is mastering the ability of reading people and a situation with more depth and insight, picking up nuances, hidden features, systematic issues, and deeply personal ones. The foreground of the minister's thinking and feeling shifts away from him- or herself and more toward people and contexts. The minister is able to take in more and more information through watching and listening; they do not immediately try to predict and control their response to the situation. Not knowing, and feeling confident in not knowing, is part of proficient practice. The practitioner is able to discern the most appropriate response, in this setting, at this time. They have moved beyond following rules and analyzing every situation to a greater capacity for seeing the whole and responding to the particular.

In Chris Scharen's first six months of serving as a pastor, he presided at twenty-two funerals, seven weddings, and thirteen baptisms, all during the autumn of the September 11, 2001, tragedies. His competence and proficiency become evident in the way that he describes being overwhelmed but in a good sense. "Even in the face of the early funerals, and despite the risk of having again and again to speak in the midst of people I did not know well, I did not feel bereft of a sense of what to do. I drew on previous pastoral experiences that had taught me how to be with someone, to listen, and to seek resources of comfort and promise in the Scriptures. Even when shaking in my boots, I nonetheless felt my way forward with a few rules of thumb to guide me."[22]

A proficient practitioner, as Scharen demonstrates, becomes increasingly wise about their own emotional stance in the situation. They can better gauge their emotions, naming and identifying how they feel, and not being swept away by feelings that could cause conflict or distract them from responding effectively in the situation. The minister is better able to be present in situations of extreme suffering and pain or crisis. There is greater emotional capacity to be with people, to be present to them. Attentiveness to the relationship becomes foremost. The minister is able to assess the situation, think about what to do and say, all the while remaining focused on the person or group.

The expert, according to Dreyfus and Dreyfus, is an even more fluid performer. The difference between the proficient and expert practitioner is that expertise embodies the full grasp of phronesis, or prudence, in practice. The minister at this level has attained a high level of thought-

---

[22] Ibid., 277–78.

in-action, though he or she need not think through every situation. The proficient practitioner, for Scharen, "does not yet have enough experience with the outcomes of a wide variety of possible responses to react automatically. The proficient performer must still decide what to do."[23] The consciousness of expert practice, then, emerges in knowing what to do without a great deal of deliberation. Of course, many expert practitioners do think through a situation but it is usually to take in new information and to reflect intuitively; their actions are more "natural" and not calculating. They are "attuned," which Benner says allows for "flexible fusion of thought, feeling, and action."[24] Expert practice is attuned to the local and particular, but this context is viewed up close and with long-range perspective. Experts can more easily grasp the bigger picture while recognizing the particularities and peculiarities of the immediate situation. In addition they are better able to identify the unexpected and respond effectively to it.

It would be my hope that every minister achieves a level of proficiency and even expertise in some area of their practice. In terms of a theology of charism and vocation, such a level of practice would demonstrate a certain attunement and rhythm with the working of the Spirit. It would mean a personal and communal recognition of the gift, formation of the gift for practice, and further honing of the gift through continued learning and reflection over many years. If we understand the Spirit's gifts as the source of the capacity for practice, we must see our acceptance and cooperation with the gift to be a necessary response. Our response is in the commitment to form the gift into a capacity that empowers good practice. Of course, the charism is not the only way the Spirit interacts with human persons; the Spirit creates and renews all of creation in an ongoing, dynamic movement in each moment of the world's existence. It is important to see the Spirit's presence as an empowering presence each day as we put into practice the gifts and capacities we have been granted. In learning, trial and error, failures, and "getting it right" the Spirit does not abandon us to our own efforts but is animating our efforts as well as intentions toward the full purpose of the gift—the service of others for the sake of God's mission.

---

[23] Ibid., 285.
[24] Patricia Benner, "Using the Dreyfus Model," 197.

The Practice of Prudence

When applied to ministry the model of developmental skill acquisition described by Dreyfus and Dreyfus helps us to see how practicing over time shapes the practitioner into a certain kind of person and practitioner: they embody an integration of knowing, doing, and being. What they do and think and who they are become more of an integrated whole over time. What kind of person do we become through sustained practice that is competent, proficient, and perhaps expert? What capacities develop in the person by virtue of such practice? What is the virtue of practice in other words?

In the Christian tradition, the virtue of practice is called prudence, and the result of long sustained practice of prudence is called wisdom.[25] When we learn something new, like how to preach a sermon, we do not possess the virtue of prudence, nor do we possess the kind of wisdom that comes from experience. A novice does not possess the wisdom born of practice and generally we do not expect them to; we look for wisdom from those who have lived, learned, and worked intently over time. But what does it mean to acquire prudence and wisdom through practice?

Prudence has long been viewed as one of the highest virtues because of its role in facilitating discernment about what to do in the concrete realities of earthly life. In particular prudence is aimed at action that is informed by both attention to general norms, values, and perspectives as well as the particularities of a situation, case, or event. It requires holding two perspectives, and, through a process of discernment called practical reasoning, a person is able to determine how best to proceed in a given situation. Prudence clearly requires knowledge of both the general and the particular, but knowledge that melds theoretical with experiential learning. A novice or advanced beginner learns how to lead worship in their tradition by following the norms of an ecclesial body but will not yet be prudent or wise in how to lead worship in all the various circumstances in which a minister finds herself. They begin by learning the basic rules and applying them to every situation. Only after

---

[25] In the moral tradition influenced by the Greek philosopher Plato, prudence is one of four key virtues (along with temperance, courage, and justice) that are necessary to develop a good society. Aristotle referred to prudence as phronesis, practical wisdom in action. Christian theologians such as Augustine and Aquinas incorporated the four moral virtues from the Greek tradition, also called the cardinal (meaning hinge) virtues, along with three theological virtues (faith, hope, and love) in their synthesis of the Christian moral life.

they have led worship in many contexts, each unique and requiring different judgment for what to do and how to proceed, will a person grow in prudence. The prudent practitioner does not apply general rules or principles without regard for the situation's particular features. The prudent person thinks, judges, and acts in a way to find the fitting course of action for the situation, which is neither perfect nor absolute in all cases.

Prudence only comes from combining what we know of the general rubrics and rules of worship with what we know of a particular community at a particular time and place. A prudent presider, in other words, not only knows the difference between presiding at a wedding and a funeral (a novice knows that difference), but also develops a refined sense of what it means to preside at the wedding of a young couple, or a couple in their sixties where one person is widowed and the other divorced. The wedding ceremony for the most part is the same, but the ways in which the presider interacts with the couple, speaks and teaches about marriage, and incorporates the families of the bride and groom are all nuanced to the particularities of the couple and their situation.

Prudence is the virtue that enables a person, according to Aquinas, to choose a course of action that is good and wise. A virtue, in his anthropology, is the power to do good that emerges from the habits and dispositions that aim toward the good and through repetitive action moves to a level of perfection.[26] Aquinas defined prudence as having eight parts that allow a person to think about their action in relationship to the situation's past (memory), the present (reason and understanding), and the future (foresight, circumspection, and caution), as well as their ability to take counsel (docility and shrewdness). Aquinas's close analysis of these parts can help to summarize some of the key ideas about professional practice in this chapter.

Memory is a part of prudence because thinking about a wise course of action includes understanding that situation's past, its context, history, and social environment. Situations are shaped by many factors particular to the people and their place, some local and others global. Memory

---

[26] Aquinas's anthropology included two kinds of virtues: virtues of the mind (intellectual virtues having to do with reason in science, art, technical matters, and *sapientia*, or wisdom) and of the will (moral virtues guiding emotions, desires, and choices). Prudence is a moral virtue that attends to the formation of the will and desires to pursue the good by making right and proper decisions in regard to particular courses of action.

serves to help us understand how a situation developed and the multiple factors that shaped the circumstance. A ministerial situation is also embedded in the Christian past, and understanding how the tradition has developed and how Christians in other times and places faced similar situations helps the minister to sort through the options for how to proceed. Knowledge of the past, according to Aquinas, is necessary "in order to take good counsel for the future."[27]

Understanding and reason are part of prudence because a minister has to consider general principles and theories that help describe and interpret the issues within a situation, some of which are apparent and others hidden or obscure. We attempt to understand the particular within a larger context and draw insight from what we know generally that might apply. This is where knowledge of theories, principles, and moral norms come into play. Because prudence is seeking right action in a particular situation, a person is not seeking a simple rule that is universally true in all situations, for such a rule does not exist according to Aquinas, but rather that truth that exists in the "majority of cases."[28]

Reason, the mind's ability to think and process information, is inquisitive and discursive. It inquires into what is the case, it seeks to describe and understand fully, and turns this understanding to a consideration of what to do, how to act, and what is the best way to proceed. Reason, in this regard, is a mental operation that is not merely technical or mechanical. Neither is reason purely speculative, contemplating truth or realities disconnected from the actual features of a practice. Reason, in the Western philosophical tradition, carries both of these meanings: thinking about technique (e.g., how do I tune a guitar?) or the realm of pure ideas (e.g., what is liturgical beauty?). Reason, in relationship to prudence, is the mind engaging in knowing, appreciating, and exploring the particular as well as the general and bringing them into dialogue with each other.

A necessary part of prudence is to take counsel, to develop the disposition to learn from other people (docility) as well as to learn from oneself (shrewdness). Docility means the prudent person is humble enough "to be ready to be taught." The prudent person is one who takes good counsel in seeking right reason applied to action and good counsel involves "research proceeding from certain things to others," which is the work

---

[27] Saint Thomas Aquinas, *Summa Theologiae*, II-II, q. 49, a. 1.
[28] Ibid.

of reason. For Aquinas prudence is involved with particular courses of action and "since such matters are of infinite variety, no one man can consider them all sufficiently; nor can this be done quickly, for it requires length of time. Hence in matters of prudence man stands in very great need of being taught by others, especially by old folk who have acquired a sane understanding of the ends in practical matters."[29] As the proverb states, "Without counsel, plans go wrong, but with many advisers they succeed" (Prov 15:22) and "Those who ignore instruction despise themselves, but those who heed admonition gain understanding" (Prov 15:32).

If docility is being able to take counsel from others, shrewdness means to take one's own counsel or "acquiring a right estimate by oneself." In this sense, Aquinas is affirming the knowledge that arises from our own experience. "We need experience to discover what is true in the majority of cases," according to Aquinas.[30] Shrewdness does not mean malicious; rather it points to astuteness, having knowledge of one's own sense of a situation, of the truth of the matter, and of what needs to be done. As the proverb states, "To get wisdom is to love oneself; to keep understanding is to prosper" (Prov 19:8). Prudence, however, is not based solely on a person's experience and judgment, which can be too narrow, for according to the proverb, "A fool takes no pleasure in understanding, but only in expressing personal opinion" (Prov 18:2).

In addition to thinking about the past, the current conditions of the situation, and of taking counsel from others and oneself, prudence requires thinking about a course of action in relationship to the future. First, it involves foresight, which means that the prudent person looks into the future to see "that to which things are directed." Actions have intention, an aim and purpose. Foresight is the ability to see what end is intended in a course of action. Circumspection refers to the means to attain that end and whether the means are good and suitable. As noted in chapter 5, Aquinas teaches that action involves what is intended as the end of action, what the aim is as well as the means they will employ to attain that end. Foresight and circumspection require that the prudent person think ahead, to imagine the consequences of various courses of action, and to choose a way that is most fitting to the situation in terms of means and end.

[29] Ibid., II-II, q. 49, a. 3.
[30] Ibid., II-II, q. 49 a. 1.

Finally Aquinas identifies caution as part of prudence. Caution refers to an awareness of the way in which good and evil are bound together in practices. In discerning a prudent course of action one must realize the way in which there "is evil mingled with good, on account of the great variety of these matters of action, wherein good is often hindered by evil, and evil has the appearance of good. Wherefore prudence needs caution, so that we may have such a grasp of good as to avoid evil."[31] As noted earlier, both our intentions and the way we carry them out are easily corruptible. The prudent person strives to maximize the most loving response while minimizing inattentiveness, selfishness and greed, and contributing to social evil and oppression.

Craig Dykstra has another name for prudence, what he calls "pastoral imagination," "the capacity to perceive, truthfully and deeply, through eyes of faith, what is actually going on in the world of which they are a part; to imagine what new life God is calling God's people to embrace; and to strengthen and enable the people to see it themselves and to live into it creatively."[32] Such imagination, like prudence, requires looking back to the past, into the present, and forward to the future in order to discern how best to live the life of discipleship. Dykstra notes that this capacity comes only through "deep and sustained engagement in pastoral work" over time. But neither prudence nor imagination is an end in itself; it is not an achievement or a goal for ministers. In fact, he notes, it is a gift. "It takes shape over time within the daily work of ministry and then somehow surprises one by its presence. As a surprising gift, pastoral imagination is like the other gifts that God showers on those who are caught up in faithful living in a variety of settings—gifts that often are especially suited to the situation and need of those who receive them."[33] The presence of prudence, or pastoral imagination, then, is like a charism, a gift born of the Spirit to build up the Body of Christ through practice.

The virtue needed at the beginning of learning ministry, or any professional practice, is patience. Learning ministry takes place over a long period of time. Some observers of professional education say it takes ten years to "become" a professional practitioner. In ministry, that means that theological education is one part of the "schooling" but that other contexts and teachers beyond the formal academy must be effective

---

[31] Ibid., II-II, q. 49, a. 8.
[32] Craig Dykstra, "Pastoral and Ecclesial Imagination," in *For Life Abundant*, 43.
[33] Ibid., 42.

places of teaching and learning. Good ministers learn ministry from other ministers as well as from the community of disciples. Growing in competence in practice takes place in the everyday work of providing care, administering budgets, planning liturgies, teaching youth, preparing a sermon, and calling for volunteers to stock the food shelf. Ministry is not six separate practices learned in isolation from each other. They can be studied and practiced each on their own, but only at the outset of learning ministry. Over time, they become one practice, melded together, flowing into and influencing each other. Vocation, as was mentioned earlier, is not three separate parts of our selves. Over time, with intention and attention, vocation becomes integrated into one life: the practices of ministry, what I do, shape and influence who I am and how I live, and each in turn, who I am and how I live, influences what I do.

Sources for Further Reading

Aristotle. *Nicomachean Ethics.* In *The Basic Works of Aristotle*, edited by Richard McKeon. New York: Random House, 1941.

Bass, Dorothy C., and Craig Dykstra, eds. *For Life Abundant: Practical Theology, Theological Education and Christian Ministry.* Grand Rapids, MI: Wm. B. Eerdmans, 2008.

Benner, Patricia. "Using the Dreyfus Model of Skill Acquisition to Describe and Interpret Skill Acquisition and Clinical Judgment in Nursing Practice and Education." *Bulletin of Science, Technology and Society* 24, no. 3 (June 2004): 188–99.

Dreyfus, Hubert L., and Stuart E. Dreyfus. *Mind Over Machine: The Power of Human Intuition and Expertise in the Era of the Computer.* New York: Free Press, 1986.

Foster, Charles R., Lisa E. Dahill, Lawrence A. Golemon, Barbara Wang Tolentino. *Educating Clergy: Teaching Practices and Pastoral Imagination.* San Francisco, CA: Jossey-Bass, 2006.

Freedman, Samuel G. *Upon This Rock: The Miracle of the Black Church.* New York: HarperCollins, 1993.

May, William F. *Beleaguered Rulers: The Public Obligation of the Professions*. Louisville, KY: Westminster John Knox Press, 2001.

Neumark, Heidi B. *Breathing Space: A Spiritual Journey in the South Bronx*. Boston, MA: Beacon Press, 2003.

Osmer, Richard R. *Practical Theology: An Introduction*. Grand Rapids, MI: Wm. B. Eerdmans, 2008.

Pieper, Joseph. *The Four Cardinal Virtues: Prudence, Fortitude, Temperance, Justice*. Notre Dame, IN: University of Notre Dame Press, 1966.

Pope, Stephen, ed. *The Ethics of Aquinas*. Washington, DC: Georgetown University Press, 2002.

Chapter 7

The Practice of the Trinity

This doctrine succeeds when it illumines God's nearness to us in Christ and the Spirit. But it fails if the divine persons are imprisoned in an intradivine realm, or if the doctrine of the Trinity is relegated to a purely formal place in speculative theology. In the end God can seem farther away than ever. Preaching and pastoral practice will have to fight a constant battle to convince us, to provide assurances, to make the case that God is indeed present among us, does indeed care for us, will indeed hear our prayer, and will be lovingly disposed to respond. If, on the other hand, we affirm that the very nature of God is to seek out the deepest possible communion and friendship with every last creature, and if through the doctrine of the Trinity we do our best to articulate the mystery of God for us, then preaching and pastoral practice will fit naturally with the particulars of the Christian life. Ecclesial life, sacramental life, ethical life, and sexual life will be seen clearly as forms of trinitarian life: living God's life with one another.[1]

Catherine Mowry LaCugna is widely recognized for her groundbreaking work on the doctrine of the Trinity in her book, *God for Us: The Trinity and Christian Life*. She argues that the Trinity's immanence and economy are one and the same: who God is in essence is what God does. Contemporary theologians like LaCugna are retrieving ancient insights into God as relationship, communion, and unity in love and mission. They also offer us a way of thinking about God in relationship to the concept of practice in fresh ways.

[1] LaCugna, *God for Us*, 411.

In this final chapter I want to explore three issues related to the practice of discipleship and ministry through the doctrine of the Trinity. First, in classical terminology Trinitarian theology addresses the immanent Trinity (God in God's self) and the economic Trinity (God in salvation history). Over the course of the tradition these two ways of talking about God as Trinity became separated, with the economic focus losing ground to the immanent. Contemporary theologians have sought to overcome this long-standing problem through a more integrated understanding of the divine life, acknowledging that the immanent and economic Trinity is one reality, not two. Who God is and what God does is one divine life. If God is one in terms of being and doing, and human persons are created *imago Dei*, contemporary Trinitarian theology offers a theological way of understanding human practice as the integration of being and doing before God. At the outset of this book, I mentioned the ancient image of God's two hands, Jesus and the Spirit. God can be known by what God does through the two persons of the Trinity and thereby we can claim something about who God is and what God does by attending to the "divine practices" of Jesus and the Spirit.

As we turn to Trinitarian language about God, I want to emphasize a second point: there are limits to human language about God, and when we use language such as "two hands" or "practices" in reference to God we are speaking in terms of metaphor and analogy in describing who God is and what God does. This is especially important when we speak of relationship and communion. We claim what we know about God from human experience, but who and what God is is always beyond this experience.

Finally, if God is a God of practice, then God is also a God of wisdom. In the previous chapter, I drew the connection between practice and wisdom and how through practice one gains the virtue of prudence, which in turn shapes the minister's identity and practice into wisdom. The Christian tradition has long recognized that prudence is the foundation of wisdom. The source of all wisdom is God and following in the path of wisdom draws us into divine life and communion. The divine source of wisdom graces the prudent practitioner with wisdom.

Trinity as Persons-in-Relationship

Most Christians know of the Trinity through prayer forms in the liturgy, such as the sign of the cross, blessings in the name of the Father, Son, and Holy Spirit, and reciting the Nicene Creed: "We believe in one

God . . ." Few can probably recount the controversies and responses formulated through the great church councils at Nicaea (325 CE), Constantinople (381 CE), Ephesus (431 CE), and Chalcedon (451 CE) that clarified the creedal formulations we repeat today. When introduced to the issues of substance, subordination, and essence we may wonder what all the fuss was about for Christians in the first centuries. The questions of that time, and their solutions, seem largely removed from our questions about God today, and yet, as LaCugna and others have shown, they are vitally important in helping us articulate a Trinitarian understanding of God for our times.

The classical doctrine of the Trinity arose from a set of pastoral concerns in the early community about the nature of salvation and what could be known and claimed about God and God's relationship to the Son and Spirit. Prior to the fourth century, Christians lived with a basic understanding of God as the source and creator of all things, as Jesus the Incarnate Word and Son of God, and the Spirit as the divine presence who guides the community in the way of Christ. We find early scriptural hints for the doctrine of the Trinity, though New Testament authors did not set down a formal teaching about the nature of God as Trinitarian; rather, they expressed what they knew about God through what God had done for them through Christ and the Spirit.

The classical formulation came out of a difference of understanding about God's relationship to Jesus. The debate arose from claims proposed by the theologian and philosopher Arius (250–336 CE). His understanding, which was widely shared at the time, is that Jesus Christ is a lesser god than God the Father, he is begotten of God, sent by God, from God, but Jesus is not God, not divine. Arius's position, known as subordinationism, is quite logical in Greek philosophical terms of the day: if God did not come from anything, is not created or generated from another source, it follows that God is eternal and immutable. If God sends the Son through the incarnation to enter history and save humanity, then the Son must be a lesser God because he is created and sent, something we cannot say about God as God. For those who opposed Arius, his case raised the question: if Jesus is not God in the same way that God is God, how could he save us? If Jesus is a lesser God, then he might make contact with God for us, but salvation is not secured through him. Only as God, only as divine, can Christ be a savior.

The first answer to the Arian challenge is the Nicene formulation that Jesus Christ is of the same substance as God, the same *homoousios*. The church recognized that Christ is begotten of the Father, from God, but not created like the rest of creation, yet that does not make him lesser than God since God and Christ share the same essence or substance. Jesus is "one in being with the Father."

The solution seemed to work despite the fact that Arianism continued to spread widely among Christians. In time, the Nicene formulation created more questions: If Christ shares the same substance as God, does God suffer? Does Christ have a human or a divine soul and mind? How is the Spirit related to God and Jesus? Debates continued and many answers were proposed and rejected. As LaCugna points out, the claim that God is one substance initiated questions about how Jesus and the Spirit share that substance and how the three exist in relationship to each other. The *homoousious* category was a way to begin to understand what God is in God's self, at the "intra-trinitarian level" and these answers formed the basis of what later was called the immanent Trinity.

The Cappadocian theologians of the late fourth century, Basil (330–79 CE), his brother Gregory of Nyssa (335–94 CE), and Gregory of Nazianzus (330–90 CE), helped to clarify how God exists as one and three: each of the divine persons is the essence of God, and the distinctions are made in terms of their relationships to one another and their origin. God the Father is unbegotten, the Son is begotten of the Father, and the Spirit proceeds from the Father through the Son. The three persons of the Trinity are equal in nature (*ousia*) and equal in participation in salvation, existing together through all time. As the Council of Alexandria (362 CE) claimed, there are three persons (*hypostases*) and one being or substance (*ousia*). The debates continued for the next century around the two natures of Christ and how the divine and human natures are related in his person.

Unfortunately from the late patristic to the modern era many of these insights about the doctrine of the Trinity fell largely out of sight in theology. When theologians talked about the Trinity, they were primarily concerned with explaining the inner life of Father, Son, and Spirit, the immanent Trinity. The economic Trinity was either discussed separately or not at all, and discussions of both Christ (Christology) and the Spirit (pneumatology) became disconnected from the Trinity. According to LaCugna, theology became concerned with articulating God in God's self, which had little connection to what was said about ethics, spirituality, or ecclesial life. The being or nature of God was separated from what God does and from what we do. Trinitarian theology was caught between distinguishing "being" and "doing," the essence of who God is as distinct from describing God's relationship to creatures and creation. There were many implications for the emphasis given to the immanent

Trinity and the loss of the economic trinity in theology. One problem has already been mentioned—that the Trinity contributed little to either Christology or pneumatology and even less to other areas of theology. Christ and the Spirit were often considered as two separate doctrines, and the Spirit eventually fell out of theological discourse, receiving only minor attention until the twentieth century.

Trinitarian thought made little headway until recently when contemporary theologians retrieved the Cappadocian fathers' insights that God is three persons who exist in relationship, a divine communion of three persons. Understanding divine being as relational and actively engaged with all the universe counters Hellenistic-influenced theology that speaks of God as immutable, distant, static, and unmovable. The insight has three important implications for what we claim about God as triune and human persons as made in the image of God.

First, the ancient formulation claims that the divine reality *in essence* is relational: the ontological reality is person-in-relationship.[2] There is not some "being" or ontological essence prior to personhood or relationship; rather person-in-relationship is the essence of who God is. The distinction between Father, Son, and Spirit is not their nature or substance but their personhood, and to be a person is essentially relational, and the distinctions between the three persons are defined by relationship. Edward Hahnenberg notes that "personhood (either Father, Son, or Spirit) depends on relationship. The Father is Father because of relationship to the Son and to the Spirit; the Son is Son because of relationship to the Father (being begotten); the Spirit is Spirit because of relationship to the Father (proceeding from)."[3] The insight of this ancient formulation is that personhood is essentially relational: relationship is not added on to being, but is constitutive of it. As Hahnenberg notes, "The divine

---

[2] A second debate, clarified at the Council of Constantinople (381) affirmed the Nicene claims and gave us the Nicene Creed, "begotten, not made, of one substance with the Father" but it was the Council of Ephesus (431 CE) that took up the question of how the divine and human natures were related in Jesus and declared that the two natures existed in a perfect union. Finally, the Council of Chalcedon (451 CE) ratified all previous councils and added the idea of one person with two natures: "one and the same Christ, Son, Lord, Only-begotten, recognized in two natures, without confusion, without change, without division, without separation; the distinction of natures being in no way annulled by the union, but rather the characteristics of each nature being preserved and coming together to form one person [*prosōpon*] and subsistence [*hypostasis*]" (see LaCugna, *God for Us*, 36–42).

[3] Hahnenberg, *Ministries*, 88–89.

nature only exists in and through persons (the divine *hypostases*)" and "only in and through relationship with the other divine persons."[4]

In explaining relationality through feminist theology categories, Elizabeth Johnson describes three aspects of the triune God: mutuality, equality, and diversity. The three persons exist in mutual self-giving and receiving. "Relationality is the principle that at once constitutes each Trinitarian person as unique and distinguishes one from another. It is only by their reciprocal and mutually exclusive relationships that the divine persons are really distinct from each other at all. Their uniqueness arises only from their *esse ad*, from their being toward the others in relation."[5] Relationality also means that the three persons exist in radical equality. They do not "lose their distinctiveness" by being in relationship, and so there are no subordinate relations within the Trinity. And the claim of three persons in one divine being points to a "community in diversity," a "*koinōnia* of mutual, equal relations of friendship." The oneness of God is not static and hierarchical, but rather dynamic and mutually self-giving. Johnson describes this communion of diverse persons through metaphors such as *perichōrēsis*, a Greek term for the movement of a wheel cycle, dancing, and the triple helix.[6] These images point to action, movement, and activity as constitutive of divine being-in-relationship.

The second implication is that claims about the essence of the Trinity as relationship-in-communion have overcome the long-standing split between the immanent and economic Trinity. The way God is in relationship to creation through Jesus Christ and the Holy Spirit (the economic Trinity) is not separate from who God is (the immanent Trinity), but one and the same reality. The ancient image of the "economy of salvation" (from the Greek *oikonomia*, the root of which is *oikos nomos*, or law or management of the household, as we saw in the discussion of stewardship) points to the idea that God oversees, cares for, orders, and is in relationship to the "household" of creation through the incarnation and the Spirit's movement. LaCugna argues that what we know of God and can claim about God is not based on metaphysical speculations about the inner workings of God (*in se*), something of which we can actually know very little. Rather, what we know about God is by virtue of what

---

[4] Ibid., 89–90.

[5] Elizabeth Johnson, *She Who Is: The Mystery of God in Feminist Theological Discourse* (New York: Crossroad, 1992), 216.

[6] Ibid., 220–21.

God has done in relationship to humanity throughout history. In other words, we know who and what God is through God's relationship to us as divine person. LaCugna writes:

> The doctrine of the Trinity, which is the specifically Christian way of speaking about God, summarizes what it means to participate in the life of God through Jesus Christ in the Spirit. The mystery of God is revealed in Christ and the Spirit as the mystery of love, the mystery of persons in communion who embrace death, sin, and all forms of alienation for the sake of life. Jesus Christ, the visible icon of the invisible God, discloses what it means to be fully personal, divine as well as human. The Spirit of God, poured into our hearts as love (Rom 5:5), gathers us together into the body of Christ, transforming us so that "we become by grace what God is by nature," namely, persons in full communion with God and with every creature. The life of God—precisely because God is triune—does not belong to God alone. God who dwells in inaccessible light and eternal glory comes to us in the face of Christ and the activity of the Holy Spirit. Because of God's outreach to the creature, God is said to be essentially relational, ecstatic, fecund, alive as passionate love.[7]

The essence of God, then, the question that the teachings on the immanent Trinity tried to answer, can be answered afresh through the economic Trinity: God is not first a God in the divine self and second a God of salvation and redemption; there is one God whose essence is relationship through persons-in-communion. Who God is and what God does are one and the same. Hahnenberg writes, "The crucial move of trinitarian theology is to claim that this *activity* expresses the very *reality* of God. God not only seeks a relationship, God lives as a dynamism of relationship, a communion of persons."[8] Johnson points to the need to understand the ontological category of "being" not as static and impersonal, but as dynamic and alive. Such a shift requires that we understand "being" as a verb rather than as a noun: "be-ing is the 'Verb' in which all beings participate, live and move and have their being."[9]

The third implication of a relational Trinitarian theology is what it says about human persons. If humanity is created *imago Dei* and God as Trinity is persons-in-communion, it follows that persons are created as

[7] LaCugna, *God for Us*, 1.
[8] Hahnenberg, *Ministries*, 85.
[9] Johnson, *She Who Is*, 239.

relational and communal *beings* that exist in relationship to all creation, humanity, and the divine Trinity. Persons are not separate, disconnected, autonomous selves, something that is largely assumed in modern cultures. Rather, a "relational ontology" points to the claim that human persons are relational *beings*. Persons are interpersonal and intersubjective, understood and known in and through relationship. There is no person who is not in relationship: we come from relationship, we live in relationship, and we live for relationship. But this does not mean that each person vanquishes in relationship. Each person is unique, claims a dignity and worthiness by virtue of being created by God. For LaCugna, a person is "an ineffable, concrete, unique, and unrepeatable ecstasis of nature."[10] Each person we encounter is a mystery, no person can be "figured out" or completely known, and yet each person is unique in terms of their origin, history, and experience. There is, in a certain sense, no end to communion and community since human persons can be infinitely known and knowable to each other.

In addition to the unique dignity of each human person, relationality points to the way in which persons are shaped by relationship and how they shape the world by being in relationship. As has been discussed in this book, the fundamental relationships of the Christian life are defined in and through the practices of discipleship and vocation. The call to discipleship is to live in relationship to God and neighbor in a particular way. The practices that constitute such a life are taken up by a community of followers who are shaped by these practices and shape the world around them in light of these practices. As persons engaged in a life of practice, discipleship is the identity and "being" of the follower of Christ, which is not a separate essence or substance, but is manifested through practices-in-relationship.

LaCugna claimed that the "doctrine of the Trinity is ultimately a practical doctrine with radical consequences for Christian life."[11] By this she means that what we claim about God impacts the way we think about our relationship to divine life and to each other. Johnson's interpretation of mutuality, equality, and diversity in community points to some of the foundational religious and ethical claims Christians make about Christian community as persons-in-relationship. She writes, "In the end, the Trinity provides a symbolic picture of totally shared life at the heart of the universe. It subverts duality into multiplicity. Mutual relationship

---

[10] LaCugna, *God for Us*, 289.
[11] Ibid., 377.

of different equals appears as the ultimate paradigm of personal and social life."[12] God's way of being in relationship points to the kind of relationality we are called to live.

Trinitarian theology also is giving shape to ecclesiology and theologies of ministry. Hahnenberg has drawn on a relational ontology to explain the distinction between the baptized and the minister. Traditional Catholic theologies of ordination were based on what is referred to as a "substance ontology," which emphasizes "particular individuals or things in themselves (substances) abstracted from their relational existence."[13] Hahnenberg and other Catholic ecclesiologists have shifted away from substance ontology to emphasize relational ontology.

For Hahnenberg, Trinitarian theology offers a way of understanding God as a communion-in-relationship that supports a relational view of the church, ministry, and ordination. As noted before, when a disciple becomes a minister they stand within the community in a new set of relationships. Ordination, as well as blessings, commissioning, and installations ritualize what Richard Gaillardetz calls "ecclesial repositioning." The change from being a disciple to becoming a minister is not only an interior change of one's self and being, nor an external change of assuming a new role or office, but a dynamic change in terms of relationships. For Hahnenberg, service is the key dynamic of this new relational reality: "I would like to suggest that ministers are not primarily isolated individuals whose relationships of service are secondary or nonessential to their existence as ministers. Instead, one becomes a minister by entering into and being established in relationships of service. In a theology of ministry, relationship—qualified as a relationship of service—is the ultimate category."

Hahnenberg argues that a relational ontology helps to explain a minister's new place within the Body of Christ. It means that who a person is is expressed in and through relationships of service. Ministers are not, as he says, "a new kind of Christian, as if her soul gained a new status, separating her from the rest of the community." Rather, "in her actions she does become something new to the community: proclaimer of the Word, teacher. . . . Her identity is based—like the distinctive identity of each person of the Trinity—on relationships. It is not simply being someone new or doing something new but a combination of both."[14] A

---

[12] Johnson, *She Who Is*, 222.
[13] Hahnenberg, *Ministries*, 92.
[14] Ibid., 94.

relational ontology holds together the importance of both "being" and "doing," both who a minister is and what they do. Neither alone can describe the full extent of ministry. A minister is not "an isolated self-identity" but neither "can they be reduced to what they do." A relational understanding of ministry, based in the Trinity, demonstrates that ministers "come to be both through what they do and who they are within the community."[15]

A relational ontology best expresses the idea that persons, created for relationship, come into being, in and through the practices embodied in community. Hahnenberg identifies service as the basis for ministerial relationships, but as I have noted it is not enough to claim service as the distinctive feature of ministry. In this book, I have claimed that ministry is a particular kind of service defined by six practices flowing from the "two hands" of God, the Spirit and Jesus. Ministry is not an action or service (for certainly many other professions could claim service as foundational to what they do). These practices arise from the very ways in which God is in relationship to disciples and ministers. In other words, the practices of discipleship and ministry have their origin in the very practices of God.

The Limits of God Language

Christians talk about God, name God, experience God, and think about God. Through language and symbol, Christians fashion words and images that allow them to speak to God and about God. Speech about God is a deeply human and religious capacity. Words for, to, and about God have a history and context; they are embedded in tradition yet never remain static. Words undergo change and critique, some lose their meaning, others take on new meanings; new words are introduced, some forgotten or rejected, and others fully integrated into prayer and theology. Christian theologians have long claimed that language for God is absolutely necessary because human persons use language in order to express their relationship to God, and yet, all language finally falls short of naming, describing, or capturing fully the divine mystery of God. God is a reality that supersedes all language, and in the event that a person or community believes they know or have named God precisely as God, they have run up against the sin of hubris and idol-making. The wise

---

[15] Ibid., 92.

person learns to call upon God by name, knowing full well the limits of their own words and voice.

Elizabeth Johnson draws three insights from classical theology in her search for contemporary feminist speech about God: divine incomprehensibility, analogical language, and the importance of many names for God. Her insights are a helpful pause and reminder about how to cautiously approach contemporary language about God as persons-in-relationship.

The starting place for understanding human language about God begins with divine incomprehensibility. As Johnson notes, it is because of who and what God is as divine mystery that humans cannot fully comprehend God. God is utterly transcendent, distinct from, and "hidden" from us. At the same time we claim that God is immanent and that we are made in God's image; God is not a reality that can be "measured, manipulated, or controlled. . . . In essence, God's unlikeness to the corporal and spiritual finite world is total. Hence human beings simply cannot understand God . . . no human concept, word, or image, all of which originate in experience of created reality, can circumscribe divine reality, nor can any human construct express with any measure of adequacy the mystery of God who is ineffable."[16]

All speech about God is exercised with this in mind: that our speech bears limits and never completely captures the reality of whom we speak. In fact, the limits of speech, Johnson notes, lead us toward a disposition of awe and adoration, so great and incomprehensible is the one who creates and loves us and who bids us to draw near. This is why she encourages us to think of language about God in terms of verbs rather than nouns: nouns can refer to what we comprehend or know, perhaps with too much exactness; verbs point to dynamic acts, to "encounter . . . that results from being sought, pursued, called upon."[17]

But, of course, we use language about God, including nouns, all the time. Thomas Aquinas taught that our names, images, stories, and concepts about God, which all come from human experience, are analogies: words that are not meant to be used in univocal or equivocal ways. In other words, when we say God is a shepherd or a friend we are not saying that God is a shepherd or a friend in the same way that people are shepherds or friends, but neither do we say that God is totally unlike what we know of shepherds or friends. Rather, the symbols are analogies,

---

[16] Johnson, *She Who Is*, 105.
[17] Ibid., 240.

they capture some truth about who God is in relationship to us, but if we understand them too literally they make God into our image.

Johnson shows how early Christian theologians described three aspects of speaking about God through analogies. First, analogies express from human life some aspect of God. There is an affirmation between a claim about God and human reality, so that what we know of God can be known through our own experience. The second move is to negate the claim: we are creatures and God is God. God is not a rock or a shepherd in the way we are shepherds, nor a father or a male or a female. Negation grasps the truth of divine incomprehensibility: "For the not-knowing that comes at the end of thought pursued to its limit is actually a deeply religious form of knowing."[18]

Out of the negation can emerge the true claim of the analogy, what might be called an "Aha" moment: "Aha, I understand now how God is my shepherd." According to Johnson, "the word is predicated of God in a super-eminent way that transcends all cognitive capabilities. . . . Every concept and symbol must go through this purifying double negation, negating the positive and then negating the negation, to assure its own legitimacy. In the process an unspeakably rich and vivifying reality is intuited while God remains incomprehensible."[19]

The third point is that human persons need many names for God. If God is incomprehensible and yet known partially through our experience and naming, the more names for God we claim and use, the more this divine mystery opens up to us and the less rigid and narrow our religious language becomes. Otherwise, we risk the danger of overly identifying with one aspect of divine life. She writes, "A proliferation of names, images and concepts each provide a different perspective into divine excellence; the diversity of the world offers fragments of beauty, goodness, truth . . . point us in different ways to the one ineffable source and goal. . . . [E]ach symbol has a unique intelligibility that adds its own significance to the small store of collected human wisdom about the divine. The tradition of the many names of God results from the genuine experience of divine mystery, and acts as a safeguard for it."[20]

Johnson's retrieval of a classical approach to contemporary God language is helpful in regard to the claims I have made in this book in several ways. First, she reminds us that all speech about God is limited

---

[18] Ibid.
[19] Ibid., 113.
[20] Ibid., 118.

and that our words, even words such as "Trinity" and "God," are not in fact God and cannot capture the reality and mystery of the divine. There is finally a mystery we cannot grasp fully, which is a kind of apophatic knowing and experience that is necessary for ministers to cultivate if their speech about God is to be true and wise.

If in fact all our speech is analogical speech about God, claims about relationship, community, and practice are analogies as well. The terms are approximations based on our experiences and ideas of each. We can speak of human relationality, community, and practice only in terms *like* that of the Trinity, but human relationships can only approximate what relationship-in-communion means; they can never fully and completely express it. We certainly experience glimpses of the fullness of divine life through contact with nature, falling in love, a family gathering, offering and receiving forgiveness, table fellowship, welcoming a new child, and so on. A great deal of life touches the divine reality and the practices of discipleship are a pathway into God's triune community. But human relationships, including discipleship and ministry, are not Trinitarian relationships; they do not express the completeness and total self-giving love of the three divine persons. Sin and failure mark human reality, and our relationships are determined in large part by the ways in which we respond to and live with the brokenness that is part of all human reality.

Johnson reminds us that any language that describes God in relationship to ministers is analogical language. God is God and ministers are ministers, but too often the two are equated. Christians have often used images of God or Jesus for ministers. For example, contemporary Catholic theology claims that the priest acts in the person of Christ the head (*in persona Christi capitis*), which draws on Paul's analogy from the Body of Christ.[21] The image points to the priest or pastor as the leader or head of the body. It falters, however, if it is the sole image to explain ordained ministry. First, it can associate the minister with the head in which thinking and reason are paramount, and the rest of the body as beneath the head or unable to think and reason. There are other images we can draw from the body, to which Jesus is also associated, to describe more fully how ministers are Christlike: stories and images of footwashing, Jesus sitting at the right hand of God, blood and water flowing from Jesus'

---

[21] See *Lumen Gentium*, n. 28, in *Vatican Council II: Volume 1, The Conciliar and Post Conciliar Documents*, ed. Austin Flannery (Northport, NY: Costello Publishing, 1996).

side, and Jesus' sacred heart. These images are also analogies for the minister: ministry involves washing feet, offering the hand of compassion, giving one's whole self and body in loving service, and cultivating a heart full of love. Images drawn from the whole body can point to the dynamic and complex way that ministers relate to Christ and the community; no single image can capture that reality.

Jesus' ministry offers a wealth of images for the minister, and I have highlighted several based on how Jesus practices ministry: preacher, healer, teacher, presider, prophet, and administrator. All these images provide ways of understanding Jesus the minister in relationship to ministry today, but even they can falter if we associate ministers with Jesus' practices and leave aside how disciples also take up the practices of Jesus. Because the practices of ministry derive from Jesus' ministry there will always be a strong relationship between what Christ does and what ministers do.

A danger arises, however, when these images are severed from discipleship or when ministers and not the baptized are associated with Christ's life and work. A relational ontology points us back to the kinds of relationships that are constituted through particular practices for the sake of the community's mission. Discipleship is a Christological reality that is rooted and grounded in the practices of Christ, and ministry takes up Jesus' practices in order that discipleship flourishes within the church's mission in the world.

Johnson helps us to see that we need multiple and diverse images of Jesus to support the full range of discipleship and ministry. No one image or idea captures all of what Christ is in the community. Any language we use about God and ministry must be affirmed, negated, and reaffirmed.

The God of Practice and the God of Wisdom

What we know of God through creation and salvation history is that God is a God of relationship, communicating and revealing God's self, in order to be united with human persons and all creation. In Karl Rahner's famous phrase, God is self-communicating love. If we can say anything about the "essence" of God, it is that God is abundant love, mercy, and grace, a God of infinite forgiveness and justice, a wildly passionate God who enters time and again into history, community, and relationship. The way in which God is in relationship to us is through the outpouring of the Spirit and the revelation of Christ.

I have introduced the concept of practice as a way of describing the integration of vocation, of who we are with what we do: we become who we are in and through what we do, and who we are shapes and influences what and how we practice. In an analogical way, we can say that we know God through God's practices: who God is is revealed in what God does, and God's practices reveal God in relationship and communion with all creation. What do we know of the "practices" of God? The basic elements of practice that were described in chapter 5 can be used here to point to aspects of God's practice. I noted that practice is an action that is about both intention and capacity or competence. In "practice" God's intentions become known to us about the full range of life from creation to eschaton: the fullness and completeness of all that God has made will come to fruition in the gift of the coming kingdom. In the course of history, God intends not to abandon humanity and creation but remains intimately involved in vivifying, creating and re-creating, healing and drawing forth; even in the midst of experiences of evil and destruction, moments of profound divine absence, the cross and resurrection point to a fundamental Christian claim that in fact God does not abandon us. In the midst of profound suffering and death, God draws out new life.

The relational understanding of the Trinity points to the communal and social basis for God's practice. God embraces time and history through the incarnation of Jesus as well as through the Spirit who gives birth to the church and blesses its members with charisms. Jesus is God's embodied practice, one whose practice is not marred by corruptibility, but is the full embrace of practice-in-relationship. The Spirit continues this embodiment in historical communities of tradition. We might say that God's practice of creating, renewing, and redeeming all of life is divine spiritual practice.

In this book I focused on the Spirit's practice of blessing human persons with charisms, gifts of service for the common good. This is certainly not the only way in which the Spirit is practicing within the world. Elizabeth Johnson's Trinitarian theology helps us to identify a much broader range of the Spirit's activity in the world and helps us to understand who God is and what God does through the biblical wisdom tradition.

The wisdom tradition offers an interpretation of the Spirit-in-practice and Jesus-in-practice through the Spirit. The wisdom literature of the Hebrew Bible—books such as Proverbs, Job, Ecclesiastes, the Song of Songs, Sirach, and the Wisdom of Solomon—is a unique part of the ancient Near Eastern tradition. This is a body of literature that does not emphasize the mighty deeds of God in relationship to the Israelites' exodus and life in the new land as does the Pentateuch, but rather uses various genres that speak to the daily realities and concerns of all human persons. Wisdom writers focus on questions of the meaning of life, suffering and death, the source and meaning of creation, justice and unjust suffering, and the ways of the wise person in a world of folly and stupidity. Wisdom literature closely examines human experience and reality and draws God into conversation about these realities. Wisdom writers did not have simple or pat answers to life's dilemmas, though there are clearly different perspectives on these questions among the biblical authors: some claiming the good prosper and are blessed by God and others challenging this point of view. Wisdom writers are searching for a way to live in the world that is good, moral, intentional, and wise.

Wisdom is not an easy term to define. Kathleen O'Connor writes:

> Wisdom is a fluid, mercurial term, difficult to pin down or to contain within set parameters. Throughout the biblical texts the Hebrew and Greek nouns for wisdom, *hokmah* and *Sophia*, refer to broadly divergent realities: to a way of thinking, to a way of living, to a body of literature, to various technical or artistic skills, to a search for meaning and order, to sagacity about life and human relations akin to "common sense," to reverent "fear of the Lord," and not least, to a woman, personified Wisdom herself. In its broadest sense wisdom is an approach to reality, an ethos which shares a set of ideas, assumptions and expectations about life. In the Ancient Near East, this way of thinking was international in origin and influence.[22]

Johnson begins her reflections on God with the "third person" of the Trinity, the Spirit, since this is the place we encounter and experience God and first come into relationship to God. The Spirit, according to Johnson, literally means "a blowing wind, a storm, a stream of air, breath in motion, or something dynamically in movement and impossible to pin down, points to the livingness of God who creates, sustains, and guides all things and cannot be confined."[23] In the Hebrew Bible, God as Spirit is identified as "ruah" meaning breath, and is associated with new life in creation; *shekinah*, meaning to dwell or dwelling within, as when God takes up residence with the people; and Sophia, the personified wisdom figure who is depicted as female and associated with female

---

[22] Kathleen M. O'Connor, *The Wisdom Literature* (Collegeville, MN: Liturgical Press, 1988), 23.

[23] Johnson, *She Who Is*, 82–83.

roles. Sophia appears in the book of Proverbs as a street preacher and prophet who announces a way of life that she is willing to offer that leads to the wisdom of God: "My child, if you accept my words and treasure up my commandments within you, making your ear attentive to wisdom and inclining your heart to understanding; if you indeed cry out for insight, and raise your voice for understanding; if you seek it like silver, and search for it as for hidden treasures—then you will understand the fear of the LORD and find the knowledge of God. For the Lord gives wisdom; from his mouth come knowledge and understanding; he stores up sound wisdom for the upright; he is a shield to those who walk blamelessly, guarding the paths of justice and preserving the way of his faithful ones" (Prov 2:1-8).

Sophia is associated with other activities and practices. In addition to street preaching, she is created "at the beginning of his work" before the earth is established and accompanies God as a "master worker" in establishing heavens, skies, seas, waters, and earth. And in this vast creative work God finds delight in Sophia-wisdom: "and I was daily his delight, rejoicing before him always, rejoicing in his inhabited world and delighting in the human race" (Prov 8:30-31). She is also a hostess in a house that she builds, setting a table, preparing food, and inviting all to come and feast with her (Prov 9:1-12). In these three great wisdom passages in the book of Proverbs, we see God's Spirit in practice through proclaiming messages, creating and playing, and eating and drinking. Within these very practices, the wisdom tradition professes God can be found. "The fear of the Lord is the beginning of wisdom, and the knowledge of the Holy One is insight" (Prov 9:10). Many of these wisdom images of spirit and Sophia are taken up in Christian interpretations of both the Spirit and Jesus.

For Johnson Spirit-Sophia points to what we mean by "God present and active in the world, as God who actually arrives and is effective where ever fragments of freedom and healing gain a foothold in the struggling world. The dialectic of the Spirit's presence and absence is known in effects—new life and energy, peace and justice, resistance and liberation, hope against hope, wisdom, courage, and all that goes with love."[24] Johnson claims that the Spirit's realm is the whole created universe and all of experience. There is no element of existence that the Spirit does not know. And because the whole world is a drama of "complexities, abundance, threat, misery and joy" it becomes "a primary

[24] Johnson, *She Who Is*, 122.

mediation of the dialectic of presence and absence" of God's Spirit. As "ruah" or breath, the Spirit is the creator of life from its inception and is ever-present in the mysteries of life and death.

But as Johnson notes, we experience this divine breath, the Spirit "drawing near and passing by," in experiences of both presence and absence. For instance, we experience the divine Spirit in the natural world through both the "Alps experience" of profound wonder at the beauty and immensity of the natural world, as well as the "Chernobyl experience," the "self-transcending protest when we are appalled at the ruination of nature and its life-giving qualities."[25] Likewise, we experience the Spirit through personal and interpersonal experience of love, friendship, trust, and celebration as well as the hurt, pain, and frustration of ruptured relationships. And finally, the Spirit works in and through macrosystems, the institutional structures that order and secure human community, which are sources of human oppression, destruction, and greed, as well as instances of human flourishing, creativity, and community.

Johnson points to four verbs that describe the Spirit "in action": vivifying, renewing and empowering, and gracing. "Vivifying" is the Spirit's creative activity in bringing forth all of creation, from its beginning as well as its continuous presence, for the Spirit "is in all things" (Wis 12:1) and "holds all things together" (Wis 1:7). The Spirit is also the source of God's "renewing and empowering" work within a world of sin, destruction, brokenness, and death. The Spirit transforms that which is marred by evil, whether in nature, interpersonal relationships, or macrosystems: all of these are arenas for the outpouring of the healing love of the Spirit, for lifting up the downtrodden and energizing prophets of hope.

The Spirit also is "gracing," what Johnson refers to as the universal offer of grace "thematized" with particular religions, communities, and traditions. In Jesus' life we see the Spirit gracing Jesus from his conception and birth; through his fasting and temptations at the outset of his ministry; in his ministry of teaching, preaching, and healing; in his suffering at the end of his life; and in the new life he experiences in the resurrected body. This same Spirit that breathes life into the world and works everywhere to bring it to wholeness is the Spirit who births and leads Jesus in his journey and through his resurrection births the church into being. As Johnson notes, charisms are manifestations of grace that

[25] Ibid., 125.

build up the Body of Christ. In all these ways, through time and history, the Spirit points to the "gracious, furious mystery of God engaged in a dialectic of presence and absence throughout the world, creating, indwelling, sustaining, resisting, recreating, challenging, guiding, liberating, completing."[26]

The wisdom tradition influenced early Christian interpretations of Jesus and several New Testament authors identify Jesus with Sophia, God's agent in the world. For example, Jesus is claimed to be with God at the creation of the world (John 1:1-18; Col 1:15; 1 Cor 8:6) and the firstborn of creation (Col 1:15). In addition, Paul proclaims that the crucified Christ is the "power of God and the wisdom of God" (1 Cor 1:24); in the Synoptic Gospels, Jesus proclaims his message in the streets, eats at table with outcasts, and takes those burdened under his wing and care.

In Jesus we experience "Sophia in action." Jesus is the incarnation of God's practices and reveals who God is and what God desires for creation through his life and death. For Johnson, the actions of Jesus-Sophia are embodied in his "preaching, ingathering, confronting, dying and rising." He is Sophia's prophet announcing the good news of salvation to all, expressed in his table manners and all his relationships. She notes that his interactions with outcasts, the poor, and women reveal the "new possibilities of relationships patterned according to the mutual services of friendship rather than domination-subordination" into the community of a discipleship of equals.[27] Jesus' death is finally a victory of love over sin and destruction, the way forward for those who place their trust in the loving divine presence. "The unfathomable depths of evil and suffering are entered into in friendship with Sophia-God, in trust that this is the path to life."[28]

Jesus reveals to humanity who and what God is, as well as who and what humanity is. Jesus is the perfect correspondence between who he is and what he does. How does Jesus reveal this? "The reality of Jesus is given in his being-from, being-with, and being-for others. To answer the question of who Jesus Christ is, we look to how he acts, to the shape of his relationships with others, with God, with the goods and creatures of the earth."[29] Jesus is a communion of human and divine, a divine gift

---

[26] Ibid., 133.
[27] Ibid., 157–58.
[28] Ibid., 159.
[29] LaCugna, *God for Us*, 293.

shared with us so that we can see both who and what God is for us and who and what we are for God. Jesus is the fullness of relationship with persons, and his personhood is constituted by "genuine freedom and communion." He gave his life completely in love so that God's love might be made known.

We can say further that Jesus, as the personification of God's wisdom, offers the path of discipleship as the way to wisdom. A life lived as an exercise of discipleship draws one into not only a set of practices that give shape to a community but also a way of knowing, doing, and being that are expressed in prudence and wisdom.

Wisdom is a kind of knowing, perhaps the most inclusive and expansive kind of knowing there is. By being inclusive, wisdom is able to discern the patterns and meaning of creation set down by God. It is also expansive insofar as it is broad and universal in scope, meaning all human persons can seek and find wisdom if they follow its paths. Wisdom is not just knowledge about how the world is made (what science can teach), or ethics (what norms to follow), or home economics (how to create a good home); rather, wisdom is a kind of knowing that arises from all sources of knowledge brought together in order to discern answers to fundamental questions: Why was the world made? What is the good life? What does it mean to live in God's ways? What is a way of harmony and peace, not evil and destruction, with creation, fellow human beings, and creatures? How are our homes expressions of God's mercy and peace?

The wisdom tradition points to the God of wisdom, and, linking this idea to the earlier discussion of the Trinity as relationship-in-communion, we can say wisdom is found within relationship-in-communion. Wisdom authors make three claims about God and wisdom. First is the recognition that God *is* wisdom. At the beginning of creation, wisdom accompanies God in bringing all of life into existence and remains as the vital energy and ordering principle of all that is. Johnson points out that as the wisdom tradition develops, Sophia becomes "a female personification of God's own being in creative and saving involvement with the world. The chief reason for arriving at this interpretation is the functional equivalence between the deeds of Sophia and those of the biblical God."[30] In the Sophia tradition, God is revealed to be wisdom itself.

---

[30] Johnson, *She Who Is*, 91.

Following the idea that God is wisdom, biblical authors attributed the characteristics of human wisdom to God. Wisdom has several key components: understanding, knowledge, counsel, and prudence. God possesses each of these in its fullness and no human person can grasp these aspects of God—they are incomprehensible, as several biblical texts attest: "With God are wisdom and strength; he has counsel and understanding" (Job 12:13); "Great is our Lord, and abundant in power; his understanding is beyond measure" (Ps 147:5); "Wisdom was created before all other things, and prudent understanding from eternity" (Sir 1:4). Wisdom also embodies prudence: "I, wisdom, live with prudence, and I attain knowledge and discretion" (Prov 8:12).

As mysterious and incomprehensible as God's wisdom is, it is not some inner essence of God that we cannot embrace. In fact, God generously shares wisdom with creation and human persons. Wisdom is a gift from God; we cannot grasp at the knowledge and understanding that is wisdom. "For the LORD gives wisdom; from his mouth come knowledge and understanding" (Prov 2:6). Human wisdom begins with what the biblical authors call the "fear of the Lord," the right relationship of awe and wonder at who God is and what God has done. "The fear of the Lord is the beginning of wisdom; all those who practice it have a good understanding" (Ps 111:10). The gift of wisdom emerges within a life of prudent practice.

Wisdom is a teacher and the wise seek her instruction. Humans long for and seek after God's wisdom, which is greater and truer than other wisdom. Wisdom calls her children to "mak[e] your ear attentive to wisdom and inclin[e] your heart to understanding" (Prov 2:2). Learning wisdom means walking in the way of God's commands: "I run the way of your commandments, for you enlarge my understanding" (Ps 119:32). It also includes praying for understanding: "Your hands have made and fashioned me; give me understanding that I may learn your commandments" (Ps 119:73). The prayer for understanding is for life: "give me understanding that I may live" (Ps 119:144). It is a prayer answered for those who seek wisdom: "Therefore I prayed, and understanding was given me; I called on God, and the spirit of wisdom came to me" (Wis 7:7).

God is also a counselor, one who offers counsel to those who seek insight in how to live. The psalmist proclaims: "I will instruct you and teach you the way you should go; I will counsel you with my eye upon you" (Ps 32:8) because "the counsel of the LORD stands forever, the thoughts of his heart to all generations" (Ps 33:11). Sophia claims that if you dwell with her and eat and drink at her table, you will find wisdom, understanding, prudence, and knowledge: "My child, be attentive to my wisdom; incline your ear to my understanding, so that you may hold on to prudence, and your lips may guard knowledge" (Prov 5:1-2).

It is clear that the fool or the evil person lacks wisdom, understanding, counsel, and prudence. They have chosen to walk another path: "the mouths of fools feed on folly" (Prov 15:14) and "a fool takes no pleasure in understanding, but only in expressing personal opinion" (Prov 18:2); and "a ruler who lacks understanding is a cruel oppressor" (Prov 28:16). Sophia proclaims that the foolish woman is "loud; she is ignorant and knows nothing" (Prov 9:13) and she draws people away from wisdom and toward death. The fool does not seek counsel, nor gain prudence in living.

Wisdom is gained through prudent choices that rely on understanding, knowledge, and counsel. It is not automatic, but comes with experience and time. It is never perfect, nor complete, since more often than not some level of corruption weakens our understanding, distorts our knowledge, turns us away from the counsel of the wise, and we become imprudent. In the wisdom tradition, the wise person and the fool are often juxtaposed to one another. Our search for wisdom, however, is probably much more a mixture of wise and prudent choices *along with* foolish and selfish ones. Prudence points to the capacity to move away from foolishness and toward wisdom one step at a time.

A focus on wisdom helps us put practice into proper perspective. The concept of practice can too easily fall into works of righteousness (I can make myself better and save myself by doing the right and good) or into kingdom building (if we work to make the world a better place, the kingdom will come). Both of these interpretations of practice are distortions when, in their extreme versions, they make human persons out to be the agents of salvation, redemption, and the eschaton. Understanding practice through wisdom places a greater emphasis on participating in a life of practices that are part of God, given by God, and drawing us into relationship with God. By becoming wise and prudent disciples and ministers, we expand the relational and communal dimension of human existence and more fully participate with God in creating, sustaining, and redeeming the world until the kingdom comes.

Human wisdom meets its limits as well. As Paul states, "For now we see in a mirror, dimly, but then we will see face to face. Now I know only in part; then I will know fully, even as I have been fully known" (1 Cor 13:12). The wisdom of practice is to stay close and faithful to practice, all the while accepting the limits of knowing and practicing. The God who exists in relationship and practice knows us fully and will bring all things to their fullness and completion.

Sources for Further Reading

Edwards, Denis. *Jesus the Wisdom of God: An Ecological Theology.* Maryknoll, NY: Orbis Books, 1995.

Johnson, Elizabeth. *She Who Is: The Mystery of God in Feminist Theological Discourse.* New York: Crossroad, 1992.

LaCugna, Catherine Mowry. *God for Us: The Trinity and Christian Life.* New York: HarperCollins, 1991.

Lefebure, Leo D. *Toward a Contemporary Wisdom Christology.* Lanham, MD: University Press of America, 1988.

Zizioulas, John D. *Communion and Otherness.* New York: T&T Clark, 2006.

Subject and Author Index

Scripture Index